Per-

Brothers Black

BRAILLE CIRCULATING LIBRARY
2700 STUART AVE.
RICHMOND, VA. 23220

Brothers Black

JAMES R. ADAIR, EDITOR

BAKER BOOK HOUSE
Grand Rapids, Michigan

ISBN: 0-8010-0054-8
Printed in the United States of America

The editor and publisher gratefully acknowledge permission to reprint the following: the Tom Skinner story, originally titled "I Preach the White Man's Religion," © 1966, *Christian Life* magazine; the Ron Williams story, from *Pacific Garden Mission News;* all other stories from the publications of Scripture Press—*Power for Living* and *Power Life* (now *FreeWay*). Thanks also goes to the authors and subjects of the stories.

To a Man Named Lilly

It is only fitting that I dedicate this book to the memory of a saintly black man I knew as Brother Lilly. Because I had known him well, Kenneth Taylor, paraphraser of *The Living Bible* but then director of Moody Press, asked me a year or two after Raymond Lilly's death to write a short biography of this legendary figure who had endeared himself to so many in metropolitan Chicago. Unhappily, because of inadequate material and inexperience at that time in the making of books, I never finished my assignment.

Until I met Brother Lilly, I, as a white native Southerner, had not intimately known a black person who shared my faith in Jesus Christ. Indeed, I had had little close contact with blacks at all.

As a child I felt warmly toward the black people. Mamie was the first Negro I remember; she worked part time as a maid in my best friend's home, and my friend Jack and I thought of Mamie, a quiet-spoken slip of a woman with a twinkle in her eye, as sort of a black Mary Poppins. To us it was a special treat to visit her shantylike home in one of the black ghettos of my hometown, Asheville, North Carolina.

I was ten when my father died; and we buried him in middle Georgia, where he had grown up on a cotton plantation. I recall that I experienced a warm feeling at the sight of several blacks who stood at the back of the church sanctuary during the funeral service, and then came to the casket to pay respects to the white man they had played with as children. I would not have been more impressed had the governor of Georgia appeared at the funeral.

Despite my affinity for blacks, I'm ashamed to say that never (to my recollection) did I strongly question during my early years why they had separate water fountains and rest rooms on our town square, why they had to ride in the back of streetcars, why black children went to an all-black school, or why indeed blacks didn't live in my neighborhood. I accepted it all as the way the world was put together, a fact of life. Now, of course, I'm glad for changes that have corrected many of the wrongs.

I grew up with vague ideas about the Negro and his religion. Somehow he seemed to have some special *in* with God. To me, blacks were good Christians, except for the black chicken thieves who sometimes raided the neighborhood chicken houses. Negro spirituals—"Swing Low, Sweet Chariot" a notable example—stirred me, especially when sung by blacks themselves.

After I began to walk with Jesus Christ as Savior and Lord in my teen years, I counted it an exceptional privilege to go with my church group to minister to blacks in one of their churches. Later the blacks ministered to us in our church and this, too, was a big event. But I never became well acquainted with any of these black Christians.

As I became more aware of differences in religious experience, I realized that blacks generally were untaught from the standpoint of Bible truth. Though many sang of "walking all over God's heaven," too few clearly knew the way through commitment to Jesus Christ. Too many were following untaught preachers who were merely appealing to their emotions and encouraging them to whoop it up in their church services.

Then Brother Lilly, a black man who knew God intimately and who had impressive evangelical credentials, came into my life in 1946. I had come to Chicago in 1945 to work with Scripture Press. A railroad man invited me to a dinner sponsored by the Christian Transportation Fellowship. Though some of my Southern brethren would have despised me for it in those days, I felt good sitting at the same table with the man Lilly, who was black as charcoal. I'm not sure why he was at the banquet, unless as a guest also: he had no transportation tie except his feet and public conveyances—the latter only when he had money for fare. During the thirties, I learned later, Lilly walked seventy blocks on numerous occasions for want of streetcar fare to minister Jesus Christ and do deeds of kindness as unofficial chaplain at Cook County Hospital, a charity institution on Chicago's near West Side. He became the hospital's first official Negro chaplain shortly after our meeting in 1946.

A tall, graying, well-constructed man who had been a carnival worker and who met Jesus Christ at a rescue mission, Lilly became a cherished friend and brother as a result of that dinner we enjoyed together. *Enjoyed* is the fitting word, too; for we shared an extra salad, the lettuce going to him and the tomatoes to me.

The love born that evening grew out of our mutual love for the Savior. I visited in his home and he in mine. I held Lilly in awe, introducing him proudly to people of my church as if he were chief of some African tribe. I saw him taller than myself as a man of God. He referred to himself as "God's little servant," delighting in giving haircuts, shaves, and toenail trims to hospital patients too poor to pay. He never accepted money, anyway; his pay was to sing and tell the Greatest Story ever told. He was so much like the gentle Savior. One of the greatest things I ever saw a man do was performed by Lilly: with strong, sensitive hands he clipped hornlike nails from the toes of an eighty-five-year-old black man who had lived alone, unable to bend over to touch his feet for twelve years! I'm honored to own a small brown, battered suitcase in which Raymond Lilly carried Gospel portions, tracts, and other items—including sample toenails, among them the tough, gnarly nails of the elderly man.

Brother Lilly (as even his wife, Roberta, called him) taught me unforgettable lessons in the art of prayer. He talked to God, not as a far-off Being, but as his dear heavenly Father, in childlike, intimate terms. At home he had a big chair beside his bed that he called the Lord's chair. In the early hours of the morning, perhaps about 2:00 A.M., he would slip from the comfort of his bed and kneel beside the chair and pray for a long time, naming patients who needed to know his Lord or who were going into surgery the next day. Tears often trickled down his ebony face as he talked to his Father about "those poor little things" at the hospital.

On October 30, 1955, God welcomed his servant Raymond Lilly (after a heart attack) to his mansion above. He was sixty-one. Roberta, his widow, took up his earthly task (see page 23). My loss was as great as if he had been a blood brother. And in a real sense we were indeed blood brothers. Despite our dissimilar coloring, we were both members of God's family through the merits of the shed blood of Jesus Christ.

So, it's to the memory of this great black man, Raymond Lilly, that I dedicate this book of stories of blacks who also are members of that great spiritual family called the Church.

Because in Jesus Christ "there is neither male nor female" (Gal. 3:28), the publisher and I chose the title *Brothers Black* despite the fact a number of "sisters" are included among the subjects. Also, men God chose to write the Bible in many instances used terms like brother, brethren, and brotherhood to include both men and women.

It is my hope that this little volume, featuring stories of blacks from many walks of life, will encourage other blacks to experience Christ as their "soul brother" and help white believers realize in a greater degree that Christ not only makes no distinction between sexes but plays no favorites according to color. Christ is the elder brother of all believers. All believers, regardless of color, are by Bible standards one in the Spirit—brothers in a true spiritual brotherhood.

James R. Adair

Wheaton, Illinois

Contents

1 Peacemaker

by MEL FLOYD

as interviewed by James R. Adair

Mel Floyd, who tells this story, was a Philadelphia patrolman until his recent retirement to engage in full-time gospel work. He was named one of the nation's outstanding policemen in 1969 at a convention of chiefs of police.

"Look, you got three guys killed in three months, and a number of kids have been stabbed and beaten. Somehow, we've got to stop all this!"

Members of Philadelphia's Morocco street gang looked at each other, then back at me. "Yeah, we really shouldn't be doing these things," they said. "But, man, there just ain't no way to stop it."

There I was, the product of a gang from this same City of Brotherly Love, trying to bring about a truce between the Moroccos and the Sixteenth and Wallace gangs.

After army duty, I had joined the Philadelphia police force in 1959. About that time, during a Billy Graham Crusade, I met Jesus Christ; and He changed my life completely. Some years later, as an after-police-duty activity, I moved with Betty, my wife, into a ghetto area to work with Bill Drury's Teen Haven organization to share the gospel with gang kids.

The Wallace guys had been warring with the

Moroccos for as long as people could remember. In time I established friendships with some of the Morocco leaders. Now I was trying to bring the two gangs together to talk about peaceful coexistence. There was no one to whom I could look for guidance except God.

At the Paris peace talks, they quarreled about the shape of the table. We didn't have that problem. We selected, without the least hassle, two picnic tables set end-to-end in Fairmont Park, a neutral area.

But getting to that peace table was not so simple. To the Morocco leaders, it was like walking up to the Vietnamese after years of warfare and saying, "Let's stop fighting."

I had rapport with leaders of both gangs. In time we got some of them together for Bible study. But for now most of our talking was on street corners, sometimes in my car, sometimes at Teen Haven.

The kids didn't hold much hope for success. "You can't get no peace. Even if you do, it won't last a week." Some guys who knew me well gave a truce a better chance: Maybe two months. . . .

One boy wanted to crash the negotiations party, saying, "Look, I'm not a chief, but my brother was killed two weeks ago, and I have a right to sit on this thing."

As the day approached for our first meeting in Fairmont Park, we had narrowed the negotiations group to about two dozen boys. We rounded up enough cars and drivers and then began to sweat and pray. Do you look for an all-out gang war, with guys drawing knives and guns, saying, "Now, I've finally got you where I want you; I'm gonna kill you"? Suppose some kid pops up and starts shooting and a few guys get killed?

Our first meeting was set for early evening. I wanted plenty of daylight. I needed to see every movement.

The agreement was that there would be no socializing or talking. So all was quiet as we sat down, the Moroccos on one side and the guys from Sixteenth and Wallace on the other.

All eyes were on me as I summarized. "We came here to stop gang fights. We're agreed on that one thing. Now here is how the meeting's going to go. Everyone is going to have an opportunity to talk, but only one man talks at a time. . . ."

All went well at that meeting—and at the two others, thanks to the Lord. It took a lot of talking, just like in Paris. We finally settled on a truce around the Fourth of July.

We agreed on a number of guidelines. Guideline No. 1 was "no socializing." We knew that gang wars developed through socializing. Say a gang member is in the wrong territory and gets drunk. Somebody reminds him of a beating or stabbing, and war breaks out. So, no socializing.

Guideline No. 2 stated that a person could walk in the other guy's turf without being molested, but he should stay out unless he had a good reason.

Our entire truce was a gentlemen's agreement. Nothing on paper. I knew these fellows well. If they tell you something, they'll live up to it—until they're highly provoked or something else happens to cause them to forget or disregard their promise.

The truce lasted seventeen months. Gang Control at police headquarters had predicted two weeks at most. But during those months I continued to work, sweat, and pray. I chased down rumors and showed the fellows that in most cases hate stories had been unfounded or exaggerated.

To keep the rapport on both sides, I'd grab eight or ten of the leaders and take them in my old station wagon to an ice cream parlor and treat them. I'd tell them what a great job they were doing to keep peace.

I'd chance on fellows with guns in hand, about to move. "One of our boys got stomped in school today," they'd say. "And nothing you say, Mel, is gonna stop us."

"Am I your friend or not?" I would counter. "When you're in trouble and you call me, do I come to the station house and take your part? Look, I don't want to see you hurt, or see somebody else hurt; you'll be in that jail and there won't be a thing I can do for you."

I worked hard to keep peace, but finally the Lord seemed to be saying, "Mel, move on. I have something else for you."

Today, the guys in the ghetto we left are much as they were before the truce—hating, fighting, stabbing, shooting, going at each other with homemade zip guns, homemade shotguns, chains, knives—you name it. It was bound to happen, conditions and the human heart being as they are.

While I don't regret working with these two rival gangs in an attempt to bring peace, I recognize more than ever that my foremost priority should be to reach blacks with the gospel. It just takes too much time and energy to do what I did. And even after you get guys living in temporary peace, what has been accomplished? It's still the flesh. If the guys drop into hell with a peace treaty, what good will that do? "For what shall it profit a man if he shall gain the whole world, and lose his own soul?" (Mark 8:36).

Currently I am on my own, under Community Crusades [P.O. Box 4252, Philadelphia, Pa. 19144].

I go with a team into black communities in various sections of Philadelphia. We show gospel films, feature singing, poetry, and plays—all in a style that appeals to our people. The whole aim is to tell them of God's salvation freely available through Jesus Christ. Knowing Him brings peace to hearts. This, to me, is the greatest kind of peace-making.

2
My Hang-up Was White People

by HENRY SOLES

as told to Stanley C. Baldwin

I was in second grade when my family moved north in the late forties from Alabama, where I was born. Southern segregation practices had already drilled into me the idea that I was not much good. At that time we blacks had to use side doors to restaurants, theaters, and other public places, and sit in the backs of buses. When we bought clothes, we just hoped they would fit and look right because no merchant would let us try them on.

In our new hometown, Plainfield, New Jersey, there was little outward racial segregation. But I quickly learned that I still had a stigma to bear. The first thing the public school did was put me back a grade. That was standard procedure for Southerners. "You dumb Southerner," my classmates would tease; and then they would mock my Southern twang.

Feelings of inferiority were only one of my hang-ups. Another was a deep-seated animosity, almost a hatred, for whites. "Your uncle was lynched by whites," my parents told me. "He was an innocent man, but he never even got a trial."

Yet, the first one who helped me change for the better academically was a white teacher. She thought I had potential. "That boy just needs to be motivated," she said. And she appointed herself to the task. Under her influence, I began to study. My grades zoomed up, and I was able to skip fifth grade altogether.

Another white teacher helped me during that period also. In class she would tell us about her former students who had become doctors and lawyers, and she'd emphasize that we could make it too.

When I was about eleven, my cousin gave me a book called *100 Amazing Facts About the Negro.* For the first time I realized that blacks had contributed much to human progress. This instilled in me a pride about my race.

But of all the people who had a part in lifting me from shame to self-respect and high aspiration, none could begin to compare with the Man I met at age fifteen.

By then I was a track enthusiast and had won medals for the 100-yard dash and relays. I also played a pretty fair piano: jazz and the blues. I'd just picked it up, starting at age five.

A cousin told me about a certain small church in our area that needed someone to play the piano. I hadn't gone to any church since I quit the Jehovah's Witnesses a year before. Man, all they did was study, and I wanted to hear some music sometimes.

The little congregation at my new church loved to travel to meetings in New York and Baltimore. It was on one of these trips to Baltimore that I met the Man who really changed my life. It was Jesus Christ. A preacher confronted me squarely with my need of Him. I trusted Christ that night, and it was the beginning of a very exciting life.

Immediately I had a new sense of worth. More than track medals or good grades, Christ made me feel I really was somebody. Nobody had to tell me that; the Holy Spirit just revealed it to me.

It was as if I'd been walking in darkness and suddenly light came. And my inferiority was not all that went. My hatred dissolved also. In its place came a great feeling of love for all people. I felt I could embrace the world. People still disturbed me sometimes; but I began to try to understand them, not just hate them.

I went home from that meeting to the same little two-room attic apartment I had left. My father, mother, sister, and I were as crowded in there as before. When we turned out the lights at night the roaches still came streaming out of their hiding places, and when we turned the lights back on we would still see them running back into the woodwork. We were as poor and had as little to eat as ever. But, though I still lived in the same humble environment, I knew I was the son of a King.

As the result of all this, I had the courage as a senior in high school to run for student mayor of Plainfield. There were almost two thousand students in school, including four hundred blacks. I was running for an office no Negro had ever won before. I got up and just spoke from my heart, and I won.

Later, after two years on a scholarship at Rutgers University, I felt God was calling me to the ministry. Inspired with a desire to win others, I organized a group called Ambassadors for Christ. We worked the streets for Jesus.

One day a man came up to me and said, "You're Mr. Soles, aren't you? I want to thank you for speaking on the street corner. About a month ago I heard you from inside an adjoining tavern. I went home that night and got on my knees and asked God to save me." Later I learned that he had been one of the biggest gamblers in town.

We also worked with people in their homes. Often they were in need of food or clothing and we would help. Then we were able to minister to them spiritually.

Over the years while I was getting my Bible training, that ministry grew. Now called the Gospel Ambassadors, it involves blacks, whites, and Puerto Ricans, who minister to dope addicts and people in all sorts of situations. Many have come to know Jesus Christ as Savior and Lord.

I also entered the field of journalism. Only one-half of 1 percent of all editorial workers in the United States are black. The *New Brunswick* (N.J.) *Daily Home News,* realizing this disparity, hired me as their first full-time black reporter.

I found newspaper journalism exciting, educational, and rewarding. I covered politics, education, demonstrations, court trials, and racial conflicts, interviewing famous personalities in entertainment, government, and business. With some I was able to share my faith in Jesus Christ.

Once my newspaper sent me on a four-day fact-finding tour to California. Filing a story via telephone three thousand miles from home was a delightful experience. Even more gratifying were the opportunities to help some little people through the power of the pen—like the family being evicted from their home with no place to go, the apartment dweller without heat on a wintry day, and the little guy who had a legitimate gripe against his local government.

Hoping to see more of my people working in journalism, I helped develop a black weekly newspaper in Plainfield. That project grew to the point that the *Wall Street Journal* and the *Plainfield Courier-News* joined with us in sponsoring an experimental journalism workshop for black youths at the local high school.

With all these activities and interests going, I didn't relish the idea of leaving my home area. However, when I saw the significant new thing Mel Banks and the others had in mind at Scripture Press in Wheaton, Illinois, I could not resist. I was to help develop and edit a whole new curriculum for the inner city!

We believed that material that used direct language, recognized the type of environment involved, and used concrete examples from the inner city could reach such youth for Christ. It was to be mainly geared to blacks, but we believed it would be effective with Puerto Ricans, Mexican-Americans, and whites as well.

The first lesson material, called *Inteen,* with a striking four-color cover, hit the market in January 1971 and was named Christian education magazine of the year by Evangelical Press Association in 1972. Urban Ministries, Inc. (9917 South Green Street, Chicago, Ill. 60643), publisher, has since introduced *Inteen Teacher* and an adult magazine, *Direction,* both of which I also edit, and more recently, *Juniorway,* geared to urban juniors. In time UMI, under the leadership of President Mel Banks and Chairman of the Board Tom Skinner, hopes to publish a full line of inner-city Sunday school material.

As I said, when I met Jesus Christ I was so filled with love I felt like I wanted to embrace the whole world. This literature won't quite do that, but I trust it will embrace a whole neglected world in the inner city with Christ's arms of love.

3
Black Samaritan

by JAMES R. ADAIR

Roberta Lilly, seventy-five, works tirelessly full time, without pay, as did her husband before her, to bring cheer, help, and the gospel to dejected patients.

The place: Cook County Hospital, Chicago, the largest charity hospital in the United States, with its 2,747 beds.

On the third floor in a crowded ward a long-term patient cocks his ear. His face brightens as he hears familiar footsteps approaching in the hallway. "She's coming!" he tells a patient in the next bed.

"How do you know?" he responds. "I don't see anyone."

"That's all right. *She's* on her way here. I know."

At the entrance to the ward, a small plain-looking black woman appears, a brown case in hand. "How is everybody today?" she says enthusiastically. "Is everybody happy?"

The woman, her kindly face beaming, walks on

into the ward. Quickly she notes that a patient here and there needs special encouragement. "Well," she exclaims, "don't tell me you're down in the dumps. Why, rise and shine and let's go! The Lord wants you to look up!"

"The sunshine lady" has arrived, and one by one patients respond to her presence. Perhaps humming the words, "Ask the Savior to help you," she goes from one patient to another. Long-term patients know that she is there to help in any way possible, and new patients soon catch on. In her brown case she has free items for those who need them: gospel tracts and booklets, hairpins, razor blades, and pencils.

Patients have different names for her: "Reverend," "Sister Lilly," "Chaplain Lilly." Mrs. Lilly is recognized as a chaplain of the huge institution on Chicago's near West Side, and has served patients and aided doctors and nurses there since 1955. Besides praying with patients, encouraging them, and sharing promises from the Bible, Roberta Lilly feeds helpless patients, passes bed pans, combs hair, runs errands, rolls patients in wheelchairs on necessary trips about the hospital.

However, her specialty—foot care—sets her apart from others who serve at the hospital. A self-taught, skilled pedicurist, she trims toenails and massages feet with an ointment that she purchases and carries in her brown case.

A surprising number of patients are admitted at County who have for one reason or another been unable to care for their toenails. Some cannot remember how many years their nails have gone untrimmed. In her years at the hospital, Mrs. Lilly has broken or worn out more than fifty heavy-duty clippers snipping gnarled, tough, hornlike nails.

Her willingness to cut toenails and care for the feet of patients reminds some of the incident in the upper room in which Christ undertook the menial foot-washing task because His disciples ignored the need.

Nurses at County are generally too busy and some say they wouldn't tackle toenails even if they had time. Many wouldn't have the strength to do the job, for it takes a better-than-average hand to snip off time toughened nails, some of which, if uncurled, would measure up to four inches long. Mrs. Lilly claims she wouldn't be able to do the job except that the hand of her God has been on her and has miraculously strengthened her hands "for this good work" (Neh. 2:18).

Mrs. Lilly inherited her hospital job from her husband, Raymond, who served County patients from 1926 till his death in 1955 (see dedication, page 5). After meeting Jesus Christ in a life-changing experience at a rescue mission, he visited one of his sisters in County Hospital and saw the needs of patients. A common laborer, he returned during his free time to clip hair, give shaves, and distribute needed items—combs, razor blades, toothbrushes, bobby pins, pencils, along with gospel tracts. Then, noticing the need of patients for foot care, he bought a pair of sturdy clippers and set to work.

Raymond Lilly became the first official Negro chaplain of the hospital in 1946, depending on the financial and prayer support of a handful of God's people as he took up full-time duties. He won perhaps an average of one hundred persons a month to Christ, besides encouraging believers.

At home his frail wife, Roberta, who had met Christ personally as a child, prayed for Raymond. They had no children. When her health permitted, she herself ventured out and visited patients in other Chicago hospitals. Sometimes she aided him in certain duties at County Hospital, feeding patients, combing their hair, singing to them, encouraging them.

Then on Sunday, October 30, 1955, at a Chicago church where he was to speak, Raymond Lilly suffered a fatal heart attack. More than twelve hundred persons paid tribute to him in funeral services at Moody Memorial Church. A great man, mightily used of God and much loved by his fellowmen, both blacks and whites, had gone to be with the Savior to whom he was so devoted. The velvety, soothing voice of Brother Lilly was no longer heard in the wards of County, and the hands that had lovingly served others had been stilled.

But the Tuesday following his burial on Saturday the frail figure of his widow emerged from the early morning darkness into the lobby of County Hospital. She had come to do what she could.

As she took up where her husband had left off, staff workers who had seen the chaplain give himself to the needs of the patients whispered, "She looks so sick and frail; she'll never live to carry on his work."

But Roberta, who had suffered strokes when she was twenty-three and thirty-one and whose lungs had always been weak, made a pact with the Lord: "You know, Lord, I can't do this work by myself; You do it through me. I'll just be the vessel; use me and give me the strength I need and I'll serve You at the hospital."

Today, ten years past the traditional retirement age of sixty-five, Mrs. Lilly is healthier than she has ever been. A hospital employee says, "Her reward for her work has been good health!" Only twice has she been off for extended periods: in 1963 for eleven days with pneumonia and in 1965 for five days when she became ill after carrying a basketful of clothes for "a little white boy" on the street because "the little fellow was so little."

Fred A. Hertwig, former superintendent of the hospital, remembering Raymond Lilly as "the epitome of dedication," once lauded the efforts of Mrs. Lilly. "Chaplain Lilly has carried on the work that Mr. Lilly was doing so well," he said, "and she likewise has done an excellent job here and is equally well thought of by everyone."

In the tradition of her husband, she arises once or twice during the night to pray for patients. Then she begins her day at 3:00 A.M. to pray further prior to reporting to the hospital about 4:45. She probably averages five hours of sleep, though she is on duty as many as fourteen hours a day.

She lives in the Senior Center half a mile from the hospital, where she has a $52.25-a-month apartment. She lives frugally, living mainly on raw vegetables, fruit juice, and sometimes wild game. ("A lady brought me some coon this week and then she brought me a rabbit; then she took me to the store and I gave 65¢ for a squirrel.") She has never drunk coffee or tea, and she's allergic to milk.

Love gifts from some of the same people and churches who supported her husband, along with a $50 Social Security pension, keep Mrs. Lilly going. People give her clothing but she gives most of it away to needy people around her.

A sizable portion of her contributions goes for the heavy-duty clippers. ("I spend more for clippers than I do on myself. The material in the clippers ain't as good as when Brother Lilly was buying clippers. They don't stand up like they should. Can't sharpen 'em more than two or three times. This week I purchased a pair for $15.98.")

Occasionally Mrs. Lilly speaks to a church group

that supports her work. She has an exhibit of shellacked toenails encased in plastic that proves (perhaps repulsively) to doubters that many people need her services.

For those individuals who support her, she sometimes writes lengthy letters from her small office in the Old Fantus Building of the hospital complex. The letter may run on and on, with little or no punctuation and words spelled as she hopes they are spelled, but the reader knows that it isn't scholarship that counts but rather the spirit of the message.

Because she shares Christ in such a practical sense, Mrs. Lilly finds many hearts open to the Savior. One man told her after he left the hospital that he was so sick he had given up, but "when I listened to your testimony my faith began to mount in the Lord." He trusted, began praying, felt God's touch on his body, and went home to share Christ with others.

Other similar cases could be recounted: patients whose ingrown nails God's little black Samaritan has operated on; patients for whom she has prayed as they faced serious surgery; people of all races, creeds, and colors whose feet and limbs she has massaged with strong fingers. All would testify that she has brought God's sunshine into their lives.

4

"Mother" George's 59 Years in Africa

by GENEVA HILGEMAN

With an alertness belying her ninety-four years, Mrs. Eliza Davis George, a spry American Negro missionary to Liberia, Africa, says, "As God permitted Joseph to be sold by his brothers into Egypt, He also permitted our ancestors to be brought to America to be sold as slaves. When Joseph's brothers came to him, he told them, 'Don't be grieved or angry with yourselves because you sold me. God sent me before you to preserve life.' If God had a purpose in letting Joseph be sold by his brothers to the Egyptians, He also had a purpose in permitting my ancestors to be brought from Africa to America. What was that purpose? In order that we might become enlightened by the gospel of Christ, and that we could then take it back to our Africa."

For fifty-nine years "Mother" George has actively fulfilled that purpose by winning her African "brothers" to Christ. Her lively spirit and quick wit let you know that she has no intention of retiring at ninety-four. The Lord willing, she fully expects to stay in Africa until He calls her home.

On January 20, 1879, Litt and Jane Davis, former slaves, welcomed into the world the third of their eleven children and called her Elizabeth (Eliza). They both had a great influence on Eliza—an influence that eventually led to her commitment to go to Africa.

After high school, Eliza attended Guadalupe College and later graduated from Central Texas College in Waco. One morning during the chapel service, the Holy Spirit revealed to her God's will—to reach her "brothers" in Africa for Christ.

Because of her outstanding Christian character and intelligence, she was asked to serve on the faculty of Central Texas College when she graduated. For five years she served, first as teacher and later as matron, while helping educate two sisters and one brother.

The time arrived when her African call could no longer be put off. She resigned from the college, stating that she was going to Africa as a missionary. College administrators vehemently opposed her desire. How could one so talented and intelligent waste her life on a foreign field? She was needed at home.

When she persisted, they asked, "How will you get funds to go? When you get there, who will support you?" Some even threatened to influence the pastors and churches against her decision.

Eliza said in her heart, "You may stand between me and the churches, but I am sure you cannot stand between me and my God!"

At a special meeting, Eliza was asked to state the reasons she was so determined to go to Africa. She presented four: (1) "I have been led by the Holy Spirit to Africa"; (2) "I have found my life work"; (3) "millions of my unsaved brethren are in Africa"; (4) "Africa is the home of my forefathers." The Lord gave her such eloquence as she elaborated on these points that some of her opponents switched to become her most enthusiastic supporters, saying it was highly dangerous for anyone to stop the movement of God in her life.

On January 20, 1914, her thirty-fifth birthday, Eliza landed in Monrovia, Liberia. She proceeded to Fortsville in Bassa County—her final destination.

Shortly after Eliza's arrival, she and Susa Taylor, her co-worker, conducted special evangelistic meetings through an interpreter. The Holy Spirit used their efforts—within two weeks 150 Liberians received Christ as Savior. The news spread quickly into the interior. Some of the aborigines wanted to have the same experience. A group of them once traveled all day and half the night to reach the place where Eliza and Miss Taylor stayed. At midnight they knocked on the door. The two women hurriedly dressed and were astounded to see the group of tribespeople.

The tribesmen begged the women to tell them about the Man who had died that they might live. At midnight the two women held a service through an interpreter. For three days they taught the tribesmen. Many received Christ, then headed home with a promise from the women to come into their area to teach.

Several months later the women received a land grant of 365 acres of forest land on which they founded and established the Bible Industrial Academy. Students took courses in agriculture and tailoring as well as in Bible.

While Miss Taylor worked at the mission, Eliza traveled up and down the dangerous river in small boats and canoes, working among the tribespeople.

In 1918 Miss Taylor, suffering frequent bouts of malaria, returned to the States. Alone, Eliza assumed the responsibility for the mission work and the care of the mission children. The heavy rainy season had begun and finding food for over fifty children had become an impossible task. The dangers of World War I kept steamers from stopping at their village to unload food. When the produce from their mission garden was used up, there was nothing left to eat. Eliza committed the problem to God. Shortly afterward she was rejoicing over the three hundred pounds of rice He had sent via two concerned men in the area.

God's love so possessed Eliza Davis that it influenced every aspect of her life. During the difficult war years she gave most of her clothes to the needy people, keeping only those she was wearing. When her dress was dirty, she had to wash it in her room, fan it over a hearth fire to dry, iron it, and put it on before she could leave the house.

When the National Baptist Convention split that year, Eliza had to seek another place in Liberia to serve. While she was considering the move to Sinoe County, one of the most difficult areas of Liberia, she met and married C. Thompson George, a civil engineer who had given up engineering to do missionary work. He had given his life to serve the Lord at the gravesite of Mrs. David Livingstone along the Zambezi River in Shupanga, East Africa. After their marriage, the Georges moved to Sinoe County.

Because of the missionary couple's deep compassion for souls, people from all parts of Liberia asked them to come to their area to teach about Christ or to send someone who could. "Mother" George, as she became known, started a national missionary movement—the Elizabeth Native Interior Mission. She trained young men and then sent them out to reach their own people with the Word of God.

In spite of the death of her husband in 1939,

Mother George continued her work. In 1945, the National Baptist Convention felt she should retire and brought her home. Knowing of the tremendous need in Africa, she could not retire. She returned as an independent missionary, carrying on the work through contributions from friends and churches.

She has spent her years not only teaching and training young men for the ministry but in actual hard labor: clearing land, digging stumps, making roads, building bridges, rice farming, building houses. To teach the people about Christ often meant walking many miles from village to village with native boys through dangerous elephant and leopard territory, during heavy rainstorms, tramping through mud, and crossing treacherous streams on slippery foot logs.

Once when she was seventy-two, Eliza fell from a slippery log headlong into a swollen river during a rainstorm. Unharmed, she quoted Proverbs 24:16, "For a just man falleth seven times, and riseth up again. . . ."

Because of Mother George's great work in Liberia, President William V. S. Tubman decorated her in 1953 with the medal of "Grand Commander for the Redemption of Africa." He also donated five hundred acres to the mission.

Many of her "adopted" children have become Liberia's leaders. One is a member of the House of Representatives, another is a professor at the University of Liberia, others are teachers, authors, and workers in high government positions. Some serve in the medical profession; others are active in church ministries.

How does Mother George feel about spending fifty-nine years in Africa? "If I had a thousand lives to live, I'd give every one of them to God for the redemption of my people in Africa!"

She wrote of her ministry in a poem titled "My African Native Brother's Voice":

And when on earth my time shall come
To stand before the King,
I'll see with Christ I did win some,
I'll hear my brother sing!

———

Shortly before publication of this book, Mrs. George wrote:

"I returned to Liberia in December 1969 to open a new area, to establish a training center for small children and care for orphan babies. I was accompanied by Mrs. Madie Lee Monroe, one of my inspired daughters of Oakland, California, who has been a co-worker with me since 1946.

"I returned to America April 15, 1970, to engage in deputation work for the new project. I returned to the field on January 5, 1972. Mrs. Monroe is now supervising this project. Having cleared five acres of land, we have built two houses for national workers. The house for children with about ten rooms is almost completed."

Mrs. George is associated with E.N.I. (Evangelistic Negro Industrial) Mission, Inc., (U.S. address) P. O. Box 8122, Emerville, Calif. 94608.

Editor

5
A Jazz Man Plays a New Tune

by CATHERINE DAMATO

The last patron drifted out of the Santa Barbara nightclub and the doors were barred on the California night. Two A.M. closing time—the hour when the entertainers relaxed. While others sat talking, drinking, unwinding before going home, the big saxophone player, Frank Mapps, sat slumped over a table, his mind clogged with booze and drugs.

"Look at Frank," someone scoffed. "Looks like he's about to die. You dead, man?"

"Frank's as good as dead," someone guffawed. "Can't keep out of trouble. Can't play that horn no more. You're dead."

But Frank did play his sax again, and he's still doing so today. Only now the former jazz player Frank Mapps plays a new tune.

Music was an important part of Frank's life since his boyhood days. When he was four in Jackson, Mississippi, his mother sang duets with him. Sometimes when in bed, little Frank would lie awake, listening to the wild night rhythms coming from a nightclub next door. During the following day, Frank would beat out the rhythm with sticks—playing from memory. He dreamed of having his own orchestra someday, and organized neighborhood playmates into a band. Using lids and tin cans, they'd march down the streets playing melodies Frank had taught them—more noise than music.

When eleven, with two broken instruments—a uke and a mandolin—he entered an amateur contest and took third prize. During the same year, he learned to play several orchestral instruments when he attended a particular church group.

Frank was sixteen in 1943 when his mother took him to Los Angeles. The big city was booming because of the war. Frank saw a saxophone in a music store next to a sign that said "Boy Wanted." He got the job, buffing and polishing musical instruments, and later bought his first saxophone to take private lessons. While there, he met Mary Dockery, who liked the way he played "Jeep's Blues." She soon became Frank's girl.

The army took him for a stint overseas in 1944. Then he was ordered to Fort Lewis, Washington, to serve in the band. Professional musicians in civilian life, the other band members showed him something new. "You really want to dig music? We'll *show* you how." Benzedrine. Marijuana. Pills. Frank tried them all, as well as alcohol.

When his honorable discharge came in 1946, he went back to Los Angeles, married Mary in 1949, and used the GI Bill to enter the Fine Arts Conservatory. There, pills weren't especially encouraged but he was taught things about the saxophone he didn't know. The urge was great to "play that horn! Make it big!" Frank finished a four-year course in three years and started getting bookings.

From '51 to '56 it was all travel—Los Angeles,

Las Vegas, Canada, the South. People liked him. He was good. And he felt good in the spotlight playing for crowds—when he had his pills.

But when he didn't have his pills, he was jumpy, irritable, and quarrelsome. In addition, the pills adversely affected his playing. And all the while something in the back of his mind nagged him. "What if the Lord calls you? Where will you be when you die?" Especially when he was alone in his hotel room, and the music was stilled and the pills were gone, these thoughts nagged him.

His big chance came in '55—a booking to play for Ella Fitzgerald. Not wanting to muff this opportunity, he prepared carefully for the performance by taking alcohol and drugs to give him confidence. When Frank was dancing around the platform just before beginning his solo, his saxophone struck a post on the bandstand, shattering the mouthpiece. Frank didn't have a spare one, so he never played for Ella Fitzgerald.

Now, a year later, in the Santa Barbara nightclub, he struggled to clear his mind.

Suddenly a seemingly audible voice came to Frank. "What are you doing here? Get out of here!" Frank snatched up his horn, staggered to his car and started the ninety-mile drive to Los Angeles. After stopping off and sleeping behind the wheel several times, he reached home about 11:00 A.M.

He went in, flicked on TV, and fell into a chair. A gospel service came on. A message on the prodigal son hit home. Frank trembled. The minister said, "Even if you have wasted your whole life, Jesus can give you new life." And there were testimonies of some former alcoholics.

When the service ended, Frank told his wife, "I believe the Lord has really saved me." Mary, discouraged by the way things were going, replied, "You'll have to prove it to me."

He took a job as a truck driver and started bringing home a regular paycheck. When his friends came around with drugs, he refused and testified to them. In another year, Mary received Christ as her Savior.

But there was the problem of Christian growth. Many of the neighborhood churches didn't honor the Word of God. There were gospel-preaching churches, but they were in distant suburbs and served largely all-white congregations. After a few months of searching, a pastor directed him to a little Bible-believing church near his home. He also learned about a nearby Bible training school. So, in 1962, he enrolled in the Los Angeles Bible Training School and graduated three years later.

When he began to understand the Bible better, conflicts developed with his employers who let him go. A chemist with a large firm encouraged him and helped him. Frank developed a detergent for cleaning concrete and started his own business, using every opportunity to witness to customers.

About this time the civil rights turmoil began to shake America, and Los Angeles had its share of strife. Frank learned that Christians were an aggressive group too. The young boys in the community needed constructive guidance, so Frank and a minister founded a boys' club with crafts, Bible study, and sports. Half the boys have since received Christ.

Frank's Bible school training spurred him on to have an active Christian outreach. A friend of his originated a home Bible class for adults and then had to leave; so Frank took over as teacher. As students began to understand the Scriptures, they became burdened for neighbors. "Christians with a Mission" began an aggressive outreach, distributing gospel tracts house to house. When the residents of Watts held a summer festival with a parade and outdoor entertainment, Frank and his band of aggressive evangelists bombarded them with tracts.

More recently Frank has been engaged in a program in Watts called the Sidewalk Sunday School. He is teaching seven sidewalk classes on Sunday mornings, using flash cards and flannelgraph Bible stories. The SSS children are given a take-home paper and a small treat. Many of these youngsters have accepted Christ as Savior.

Experiences have been varied since Frank played for the "big time." He still plays his saxophone—but the music that comes out has more of a heavenly sound. He says, "When I was trying to make the big time, I thought that music would satisfy my heart; but all the while I was empty. Now the Lord Jesus has filled that emptiness and given me something really worth playing about!"

6

He Helps Shape a Nation's Destiny

by TOM WATSON, JR.

When Aaron Gamede received an honorary LL.D. degree at Wheaton (Illinois) College in June 1968, a unique cycle was completed. The event probably did not attract wide attention in the academic world, but it was a demonstration of the practical value of a foreign mission ministry—the fulfillment of something that started in the early 1890s when Malla Moe, working under the Scandinavian Alliance Mission, began a pioneer work in Swaziland.

One of the Swedish woman's first converts was Gamede's father, himself only a youth at that time. Under the faithful instruction of Miss Moe and the other missionaries of the organization now known as TEAM, the semiliterate Swazi grew into a useful man of God who led his own family in the path of righteousness.

Somehow young Aaron managed to resist making a commitment to Christ until he was nineteen, but his was a full surrender to God for whatever service he could render among his people. He began with the opportunity nearest at hand—a group of herd boys only a few years younger than himself. He taught them to read and did his best to lead them to faith in Christ.

Aaron completed teacher training in TEAM's Swaziland schools, and embarked immediately on a career as a teacher. But as doors opened more widely before him, he realized that he must equip himself more thoroughly.

The idea of going to the United States seemed an impossible dream, but by this time the determined young Christian had lost his fear of apparent impossibilities. In 1947 his dream was realized, and he arrived on the campus of Wheaton College.

Several years later, when Aaron returned to Swaziland, he held a master's degree in Christian education—and had won a host of friends and prayer helpers in America.

For more than five years Gamede edited an evangelical magazine called *Africa's Hope*. He was ordained a minister in the Bantu Evangelical Church. Next he served as a lecturer in Biblical studies at South Africa's University of Fort Hare. Then he accepted the appointment of his church to administer the schools the missionary society was turning over to nationals.

In 1965, unexpected recognition came from the monarch of the then British protectorate. King Sobhuza II asked Gamede to serve as senior liaison officer in negotiations between the Swazi and British governments for independence. It proved to be God's call for the fervent Christian to move into a place of prominence and leadership among his people. Two years later Sobhuza appointed him a senator in the newly formed parliament, and only a month later named Gamede minister of education. Currently he is High Commissioner of Swaziland to Great Britain and several other European countries, a post equivalent to ambassador.

On Sept. 6, 1968, Swaziland officially joined the ranks of Africa's emerging nations as a constitutional monarchy, with King Sobhuza heading the government. His cabinet—including Gamede, two houses of parliament, and the Swazi National Council help guide the destiny of the self-governing state. Swaziland is a member of the British Commonwealth and of the United Nations. It stands firmly among the African nations that reject Communism and cooperate with the United States. But this accomplishment did not take place without a struggle—or without the dedicated and skillful diplomacy of Aaron Gamede and his discerning use of what the Swazis call "the vision of Somhlo."

Somhlo—the first king of the primitive African tribe—saw in a dream a great ship approaching the shore of his country bearing several white people. One held out a book in his right hand and a coin in his left. The king considered the dream a revelation from God. He interpreted it to mean that whites would come offering two opposing ways of life—one based on a book, the other based on a materialistic philosophy. Since the book was held in the right hand, the Swazis concluded that they should follow the white man who brought them a book. When missionaries later came with the Word of God, they were welcomed. The Bible was accepted officially and made the basis for the social and political philosophies of the Swazis.

"But the exact interpretation of the coin remained a mystery," Gamede explains. "The people understood what they had accepted in the Word of God, but they were not sure what it was they had rejected—what was represented by the coin. Everyone recognizes that capital and materials have their legitimate place in life. We use money in Swaziland like everyone else. As our governmental system began to take shape in preparation for our independence, there were political parties and leaders who were influenced by Communists. Their interpretation of Somhlo's vision was that in rejecting the coin the king had rejected capitalism.

"This was a difficult point to refute—at least until I realized that a better theory on the meaning of the coin was that of atheistic materialism—the very opposite from the meaning of the Book, the Bible. I pointed this out to our king and to the men responsible for the designing of our government. Some shrugged their shoulders—but happily many listened. As a result, ours is a government that accepts the authority of the Word of God and is not aligned with atheistic Communistic countries."

Who, then, is better qualified than Aaron Gamede—a distinguished product of Christian missions—to speak of the future of the missionary enterprise in Africa? As an evangelical believer, the High Commissioner looks forward with profound optimism, just as he looks backward with gratitude.

"I feel that the impact the Christian missionaries have made in Swaziland has been remarkable, and can be judged in two ways. The spiritual impact is not immediately visible to the visitor until he has been in our country long enough to see what has been accomplished. But immediately visible to any visitor are the schools, hospitals, and other forms of social service developed by missionaries.

"These types of missionary service have greatly enriched the lives of our people.

"I think there is a good future for missionaries in Africa," Gamede continues. "When 'independence fever' caught Africa there was a reaction against colonialism which tended to involve missionaries.

Some looked upon this as a closed door to the gospel, but that is not the case. It called for a change in attitude and approach. There are no closed doors for missionaries who accept Africans as equals. The role of missionaries now will be to train African leaders. Missionaries will help nationals achieve national-set goals!"

Meanwhile, Dr. Aaron Gamede is not waiting for someone else to do what he himself is capable of doing alone. When affairs of state are completed for the day, he works on a Swazi translation of the Bible. It is one more effort on the part of this dedicated public servant to bring his people another step closer to their national destiny—and to God.

7

Amtracker on Track for God

by JAMES R. ADAIR

When flood waters surged over parts of the upper Midwest for a month in midspring 1969, the Northern Pacific's *North Coast Limited* couldn't crack the water barrier, separating dining car waiter Tommy Morris from another job in Chicago.

Figuratively, nothing short of high water stops Tommy from reporting for his Chicago job, though he receives no remuneration for his work. His is a volunteer job for the Lord. When his train, now under Amtrack and named the *Burlington Northern Empire Builder,* grinds to a stop periodically in Chicago's Union Station, after its run from Seattle, he checks into a hotel, then hikes to the famous Pacific Garden Mission. Here for an evening and a morning—before he leaves Chicago—he takes up a role familiar to him for many years: serving the Bread of Life to spiritually hungry people.

From his Bible, he counsels GIs in the mission's servicemen's center; he serves as personal worker in the prayer room following gospel services for Skid Row wanderers, and occasionally goes out on follow-up assignments in residential districts.

Though he enjoys serving savory specialties on the *Empire Builder*, Tommy Morris gets an even deeper satisfaction sharing life-giving food for the soul.

One of Tommy's happiest experiences occurred some years ago in Seattle, at the other end of his run. One Sunday morning, unable to go to church because he finished work late, he decided to take his Bible and gospel tracts to a street corner. He'd pass out tracts and go to a 3:00 P.M. service. "I stood there on the corner and I froze—for some reason I couldn't pass out a tract," Tommy recalls. "So finally I started walking—where, I didn't know. About the middle of a block a white man stopped me. He said he was hungry. He was out of the penitentiary after twenty years. 'I can't get a job,' he said. 'Nobody cares about me.' He broke down and cried. 'I'm just ready to give up. Can you help me?'"

Tommy said he didn't have money to give, but that he would take him into a restaurant and buy him dinner. As the man dined, Tommy counseled, "I want to tell you about a Friend who sticks closer than a brother. I'm going to tell you whom you should turn to in this hour. I don't care what you've done—man may fail you but the Lord Jesus Christ shed His blood for you to save you if you'll let Him inside your heart."

The ex-prisoner listened as Tommy talked further, but made no positive response. After giving him a tract, Tommy left him in the restaurant. Returning to the street corner, he found perfect freedom now in distributing tracts. Presently, he looked up and here was the ex-prisoner again. After further conversation, Tommy took the man to Bread of Life Mission. Here the man heard a gospel message, responded to the invitation, and Tommy counseled him in the prayer room. He made a commitment to Christ. Tommy realized how definitely he had been led of the Holy Spirit that morning when the man later testified in a mission service, "I was on my way to commit suicide when a Negro man spoke to me and brought me in and pointed me to the Savior."

Born in 1911 in Keokuk, Iowa, Tommy Morris lost his father and mother early in life; and he and a younger brother went to live with an uncle and aunt. The uncle was a minister and Tommy received Christian training.

But, nevertheless, he began to serve Satan after finishing high school. As a boy he had played a snare drum his mother gave him, so he got a job as a trap drummer in a syncopating orchestra. As the years passed he played for Ted Williams and his Golden Pheasant Orchestra, Ed Woods and his Greyhounds, and Cecil Bruton and his Blue Rhythm Kings.

The more he beat out tunes the deeper he got into sin. "I went down and down," says Tommy. "I married in 1939 and I didn't marry in the Lord. We had spent much time drinking together."

Finally, after the birth of a daughter, Janice, Tommy's wife, Hazel, who had professed faith in Christ in her early years, renewed her fellowship with the Lord in a Nazarene camp meeting. Then she became burdened for the salvation of her husband, but he gave her little encouragement.

On Palm Sunday 1949, arriving home from his rail run, Tommy announced that he was going to bed. But persistent Hazel convinced him that he should go to church. She and the pastor had been praying for him with increased fervor.

Tommy says he can't remember the pastor's

message, but he became convinced of his sinful life. Tears rolled down his cheeks as the invitation was sung. "This was the first time I saw myself as a sinner before God, on my way to eternal damnation. My heart was heavy," he remembers. "All I could do was to cry out, 'O God, O God.' "

The pastor came and put an arm around Tommy and urged him to say yes to Jesus Christ. But it wasn't until afternoon, at home beside his bed, that Tommy finally opened his heart to the Savior.

Yet for months afterward, in church services, his old sins came back to haunt him. As invitations were given, he wept. "I don't know whether the Lord has really forgiven me," he once sobbed to his wife.

"What did you tell the Lord?" Hazel countered.

"I asked Him to forgive me for my sins. I asked Christ to come into my heart."

"All right, if you did that, what did the Lord say He'd do? Daddy, you've got to make up your mind now whether you're going to believe Satan or God."

Tommy Morris saw his salvation in a new light from that time on. His pastor helped him get established in the Bible. He took correspondence courses from Moody Bible Institute and Northwestern Bible School.

Meantime, he became active in soul-winning at both ends of his North Coast Limited run—in Seattle and Chicago. Then came an invitation to pastor floundering St. Mark's AME Church, Duluth, Minnesota, once the third largest in its district. Because he got only $50 a month, Tommy continued railroading, with the Sunday school superintendent preaching when Tommy was forced to be away. When the church grew to the point of being able to support a full-time minister, Tommy resigned and once again began moonlighting for

God in Chicago and Seattle. That was more than four years ago.

But nevertheless, Tommy Morris finds occasions —other than at the end of runs—to preach. Take the time his train was derailed in Fargo, North Dakota. Suffering a fractured vertebra, he was hospitalized for eight days. On Sunday morning, when he had planned to be in church, God began arranging things. Someone noticed his Bible, and "one word led to another," as cheerful, beaming Tommy recalls. Soon nurses and others filled the room, and Tommy was sitting up "with my Bible preaching Christ." Tears came to a few eyes. "Pastor, this is what we need." "Oh, if only we got this message in our church." Along with comments came plants and cards and gifts.

Yes, Tommy Morris believes in being on the job for Christ—as well as for Amtrack.

8
Willie Bush: Navy Cook

by NEIL G. CAREY

This account originally appeared as an "Unforgettable Person" story in Power, *the forerunner of* Power for Living. *Though it pertains to the 1950s, it is included to show the influence of a black man on the crew of a navy ship.*

God sent Willie Bush to the destroyer U.S.S. *Theodore E. Chandler* on which I was gunnery officer in thrilling answer to prayer, I believe.

It was November 1952, in the third year of the Korean War, and my destroyer was scheduled for a third cruise to Korean waters. To me, the prospect was frightening—not because of the military dangers but because of the sailors' wild abandonment to immorality that I had seen in foreign ports on an earlier trip. Our ship needed a powerful Christian testimony; and my wife, Betty, and I prayed together for the arrival of such a Christian sailor as the ship rode at anchor in San Diego harbor.

I was willing to be a shipboard witness for Christ, but my rank of lieutenant prevented me from getting next to the enlisted men like another sailor could do.

We had asked God specifically to send sailors to the ship who were steeped in Bible knowledge through memorization work with the Navigators, whose Bible correspondence course is specially slanted to navy men. We tried to imagine such fellows sprinkled about the ship witnessing as they worked.

As the day drew near for the ship to weigh anchor, it was evident that there was not one Navigator equipped fellow in the crew and certainly none among the officers. I remember Betty quoting Matthew 9:37, "The harvest truly is plenteous, but the laborers are few. . . ."

At the last minute several new men came aboard. They excited little comment as duty changes are frequent. If I only had known what was in store for the ship, besides good food, from the new man that took over the officers' wardroom pantry, I might have upset ship routine with a thunderous "hallelujah."

The roasts that began to appear on the wardroom table, the baked hams criss-crossed and spiced and sporting pineapple rings like those in magazine pictures, the brown turkeys and fried chicken, and even the scallops stirred comment and strengthened the morale of the officers leaving port for a third tour of Korean duty. We were in excellent humor, meal after meal, and this good feeling spread out on the crew.

I don't suppose there was one of the twenty-one officers who didn't pause at the galley door some time or other to compliment Willie Bush, the new six-foot, muscular Negro cook in his white apron. I stood fascinated one day watching him bone a ham. His skill was wonderful to see. The captain joined us in free and high praise of the new cook.

So we all came to know Willie as a conscientious, intelligent, polite, and hard-working navy man, first rate at his particular job. But we learned that he ranked another job ahead of his culinary exploits—that of telling the crew about his Savior and Lord. In his quiet, poised way, he never let anyone stand long in doubt of his surrender to Christ. There wasn't a man on board who had more respect from his fellows than Willie.

I don't know how much it had to do with Willie's subsequent action, but one day I asked him how he felt about I Peter 2:15, "For so is the will of God, that with well doing ye may put to silence the ignorance of foolish men. . . ."

Soon after that Willie asked the captain for permission to hold Bible study classes each Wednesday and Sunday evening. The captain was dumfounded. Never in his navy career had a sailor offered himself as a Bible teacher aboard ship. I hadn't heard of it in my thirteen years in the service, either. The chaplain said he was too busy with other things on eight destroyers, and he would have nothing to do with it.

Willie had prayed before he approached the captain, I learned. The Lord had laid it on his heart one night, alone at sea, to teach the Bible to sailors. The captain was heartily cooperative. A notice, printed in the ship's plan of the day, brought the news to every man on the ship.

Without supernatural courage, Willie Bush might have backed away from this enterprise for many reasons: extremes of inertia and resistance from unsaved and backslidden crew members; his own race and rate and fifth-grade education; the discouragement of worldly chaplains; and the strenuous tasks of a cook's long hours. But the devil got no foothold.

Each Wednesday and Sunday we were reminded anew of the Bible class by notices in the plan of the day, and by announcements over the loudspeakers. The officers heard it too. "There will be

Protestant lay service in the forward diesel at 1930." (That's navy jargon for 7:30 P.M.)

Naturally there were jibes and jokes about those "catacomb Christians" crawling into the forward diesel engine room to pray. Attendance fluctuated between six and ten regulars. Singing was loud and joyous as men picked their favorite hymns.

Just before bringing their petitions to the throne of grace, they all joined in singing "Sweet Hour of Prayer." Then they prayed for unsaved shipmates, wives and children under hardship, preachers and missionaries everywhere, navy chaplains, Koreans, special requests, and illnesses.

Bible study started with Matthew, progressing slowly through the four Gospels. This continued as the ship moved in and bombarded North Korea. Each month we had a few days in port: Hong Kong, Sasebo, Yokosuka, Beppu. Each time that we anchored or secured alongside a tender for new supplies in Asiatic ports, prayers were more earnest for God to provide the way out of temptation for all the fellows.

Discussion in the Bible class was practical. A frequent subject concerned Christ's many resistances to temptation. "Why did Jesus have to be tempted so much?" "Why is sin in the world at all?" Questions came back thick and fast at times, sailor to sailor. Those sailors had been months away from home and had been up against the powerful enticements of foreign ports. We often heard, "What's the difference? Nobody at home will ever know."

Willie Bush always opened the Book. "All your answers are here. Ask the Holy Spirit to help you find the answers in God's Word. Just give yourself completely to my Lord Jesus Christ, and He will give you victory over sin. The God who can make the heavens and the earth can certainly smooth out your troubles."

Bush and the Bible class proved their value to individuals and to our country. Our destroyer went back to the line in the Sea of Japan with the cleanest health and highest morale record in the division. We had fewer cases of venereal disease than any of the other destroyers, and our brig was empty.

Bush seldom set foot on the "beach." It held no lure for him. His interest spanned thousands of miles to his home in the States where his wife, Lillian, and four children—Ernestine, Patricia, Lucinda, and Jerry Alexander—awaited him.

In March 1953, I learned that God had opened the way for my wife to sail to Japan. Our boys stayed on the Michigan farm with their grandmother. A month later, Betty was in Yokosuka and came aboard the ship for dinner. She had gospel tracts for everyone.

She heard a lot of talk about our bombardments, six gun salvos, rocking and rolling of the "tin can," lights knocked out, and dust and dirt showering down from the overheads and bulkheads, but her one curiosity was to see where the unusual Willie Bush cooked during this rugged activity.

We squeezed into the officers' pantry. The whole space was six by ten feet but only part of this provided standing room. A 30-inch stainless steel counter ran port to starboard along the wall next the wardroom and a big refrigerator, lockers for canned goods and spices, and canisters for flour, sugar, and coffee took up more space. (Bush did his roasting and baking in the kitchen galley.) Even a stool was excess gear, so the workers ate all meals standing at the counter. Four men worked in the pantry. Bush and an assistant prepared food, and two stewards waited on table.

Betty was amazed that Bush produced excellent meals in these cramped quarters, in port or at sea, never getting flustered, never growling. Officers' stewards and cooks have long hours, too, because of the late dinner hour in the wardroom and the early morning cleanup of the litter left by those on night watches.

Betty and Bush had a long talk about his home and family. He was born in Buford, South Carolina, in 1925 where his father farmed. He had to go to work on a construction gang after finishing the fifth grade. Betty was amazed, for she had decided Bush was at least a junior college graduate. Bush says he got most of his education right from the Bible. The Selective Service draft whisked Bush away from his home and family, but he was determined to make the best of it.

"God used a lot of Christians to bring me to a decision," Willie related. "It finally happened two years after I joined the navy, at Bethel Baptist Church in San Diego. That church makes a real effort to welcome and bring in the servicemen, sending notices to the ships and the boot camp. There are 150 or more servicemen in the life of the church."

Bush thanks the Lord for the prayers of his Christian mother and his childhood friend Lillian, who became his wife, and for radio evangelists and Bible study which helped him on the way.

At sea, traveling around and seeing how some people "carry on," Bush realized the need for every Christian to bring God's Word to the hearing of the unsaved. "They can't get goodness by themselves. It's Christ in us that does it all, and more prayer of Christians is all that will change the world," is Bush's conviction.

Then came that night alone at sea when the Lord laid it on his heart to teach the Bible. Our ship was not the first on which Bush had classes, and I feel sure it won't be the last. He was assigned to another destroyer when our ship hit San Diego, and, without grumbling about not being allowed to see his wife and new baby, Willie Ann, in Coronado, cheerfully obeyed orders.

I left the navy shortly after that and set about carving a civilian career. Betty learned by visiting Mrs. Bush that Willie may stay on in the navy. If so, I know it must be because he feels God has work for him to do among sailors. I know just how much personal sacrifice that decision would mean for Willie and his family, but he and his wife are willing to make it. Maybe even now Willie is the answer to another fervent prayer rising from Uncle Sam's fleet on behalf of some tough crew.

In my navy experience, Willie Bush is unforgettable. I have been shamed and inspired by his example to pitch in for our Lord and Savior as I never did before. It would be impossible to count the other sailors who have been goaded and will gird themselves to do a better job because of Willie Bush, navy cook.

9
God's Gazelle

by GORDON C. TIMYAN

"I love to run . . . and being a loyal Kenyan, I run for my country, but deep inside I run for God." One of the greatest distance runners of all time, Kip Keino of Kenya was gracious as we chatted across the table in an African hotel lobby. I could hardly believe that we had only met the day before, for he talked as easily as an old friend. He often flashed a quick smile that lit up his black eyes and occasionally he broke into a wide grin. Keino spoke excellent English as he quietly told of his brilliant international career as a track star. It was with real warmth that he introduced me to his younger running mate, Ben Jipcho, and told me how much it meant to him to have a Christian brother on the Kenya track team.

He offered his own Christian testimony: "Before each race I pray alone in my room. Then I'm ready to go out and run my best on the track." His love for the things of God was apparent as he talked with enthusiasm of a city-wide evangelistic effort in Nairobi. Then this very affable young man, whose name had suddenly flashed into the headlines when he broke the world's 3,000- and 5,000-meter records in one year, recalled his humble beginnings.

"I grew up in the steep hills of Kalenjin country [in western Kenya], where for a time I was a herd boy for my uncle's goats," he began. "And I know how frightened a young boy can be when he looks through the bushes and finds a snarling leopard crouching over a goat he has just killed. I think I had my first lesson in running a race that day. And I didn't look back!" he added with a grin. He went on to tell how the loss of his mother early in life had brought hardships. He was shifted around between his grandmother, his father, and his uncle. It had been a real struggle to secure a primary school education. Even his own father opposed him, but young Kip's pleading finally won out. Once Kip was enrolled in school and began to compete in sports, his father's opinion changed completely. Since he himself had been an outstanding runner in his younger days, the elder Keino encouraged his son to develop running abilities. This led to his being placed in a police training college, where there were athletic facilities.

As I admired the slender but sturdy physique of a natural athlete, I was amazed that his height was only 5′ 9″, and that he weighed only 145 pounds. He had seemed much taller to me as I watched his smooth-flowing gait on the track the day before. He had moved past some of Africa's best with the greatest of ease. Perhaps it was because Kip's legs are extra long—a Kalenjin tribal characteristic—that his length of stride is longer than average for even an African. I know it was pure poetry to see him in motion. Like a gazelle bounding across the savannahs, I thought, as I watched with admiration his beautiful style. With no formal training, Keino had conditioned his lithe body into a superb running machine and had shown the world a fierce determination to win.

But Keino was still an unknown police inspector from Kenya when he warmed up for the 5,000-meter race at Helsinki in the World Games of 1965. He told his manager, "I'm going in and try my level best by going full out!"

The two top distance runners in the world were there, Michel Jazy of France and Ron Clarke of Australia, plus a large field of lesser known athletes.

From the outset of the 5,000 meters Jazy and Clarke battled for the lead with England's Mike Wiggs and Kip Keino. The front four pulled away from the rest of the field. All eyes were on the two stars at lap six, but to their amazement the smooth-striding Kenyan stayed right with them. Sensing that an upset was in the making, the crowd broke into a spontaneous chant, "Keino! Keino!" and then, "Keino! Kenya! Keino! Kenya!" The young African heard his name shouted by a foreign crowd for the first time and was spurred on.

As they entered the final lap, Jazy and the Kenyan both shot ahead of the Aussie champion Clarke, bringing the thirty-two thousand spectators to their feet with a roar. Keino ran neck and neck with the great Jazy until in a final burst of speed the Frenchman broke the tape a scant yard ahead of him. But the unheralded Keino had defeated Ron Clarke and had given the proud French champion a real scare. He had gone "full out" and for the first time in his running career, found that he had a finishing kick. He made up his mind that day that he could and would improve his sprint until he became a world record holder. It had been a tough training grind on a mountainous course in Kenya that he and his colleagues called "Agony Hill," but it had been worth it!

At another Finnish meet in Turk, three days later, Keino beat Ron Clarke for the second time. With four laps to go, Clarke stepped up the torrid pace he had maintained but still he couldn't shake off his African rival. The "Kenyan Gazelle" streaked down the straightaway in a superhuman effort that carried him past the champ and lifted him into world fame. He had beaten Clarke by three seconds, ran the best race of his career, and missed the world record by only four-tenths of a second on a soggy track. Under the right conditions, he knew he could break that record.

A week later Keino was the star attraction at Stockholm. The stadium was packed with spectators who hoped to see him set the world record and defeat titlist Ron Clarke for the third time. At the seventh lap Keino pushed past Clarke. The voice of the crowd rose in a crescendo, "Keino! Kenya!" as their idol set a fast pace with Clarke following close behind.

Then Kip put on a tremendous burst as the tape came into view. But as he broke the tape well ahead of Clarke and prepared to leave the track, he was startled to see Clarke flash by him! The officials beckoned him to continue. He realized instantly that the race was not over, but it was too late to catch Clarke. What had happened? None of the Kenya team had understood the announcement in Swedish that a three-mile tape had been placed near the end of the 5,000-meter course just in case another record might be broken during the longer race. In fact, he *had* broken the three-mile record unofficially and most observers felt the 5,000-meter mark would have fallen too if Kip's stride had not been broken. Kip had goofed, and he knew it!

It was a great disappointment to him. He felt bitter about the misunderstanding concerning the two tapes. He was resentful of Clarke's allowing him to set the pace. The Aussie had said publicly, "It was a bit unfair of me to make Kip set the pace. Had we shared the lead, he might have broken the record." Though his own error was hard for him to take, Kip had learned by now to ask God to remove the bitterness from his heart. Now he was to learn to accept himself. He publicly admitted his mistake to the press and sportingly granted that "Ron Clarke was coming up so fast that he probably would have beaten me anyway." Where had he found the secret that enabled him to overcome his initial bitterness, accept himself despite his own error, and forgive his rival?

Two years before, in January 1963, Keino had married a school chum, Jane Jepketer. She was the daughter of a devout Christian Kalenjin tribesman. His new father-in-law, Arap Tigor, faithfully observed Bible reading in his home and had been encouraging Keino to do the same in his new marriage relationship. Often until late at night the old man would explain difficult passages of Scripture to the skeptical Kip, weaving in God's plan of salvation.

One day as they were discussing the tenth chapter of Romans, the Bible spoke to Keino personally, "that if thou shalt confess with thy mouth the Lord Jesus and shalt believe in thine heart that God hath raised him from the dead, thou shalt be saved." That day Keino found new life in Christ. No wonder he could find forgiveness for himself and for Ron Clarke and take on a positive attitude as he looked forward to his next race.

Seven weeks after having lost at Helsinki, he broke his first world record. It was August 27,

1965, in Halsingborg, Sweden. The plan for the 3,000-meter race came to him in the hotel the night before. He figured each lap would have to average 63 seconds to break the mark. He committed the race to God, then retired to sleep soundly. The next morning he rechecked his figures, told his coach of his plan, and executed it perfectly that afternoon. His long legs working like well-oiled pistons carried him to victory, breaking the old record by 6.5 seconds. He had set his first world mark! Then three months later he captured his most coveted record—the 5,000-meter—in Auckland, New Zealand. There he beat Ron Clarke's world mark by 1.6 seconds.

Through the months that followed these world records in the longer distances and the added honor of becoming Africa's first runner to break the four-minute mile, Keino was lionized wherever he went. When he returned to his Kenyan Police Training School in an open Land Rover, the approach to the college was lined by hundreds of cheering policemen Kip was uncomfortable with all these formal honors, for his modesty made him shy away from hero worship. He was never an aloof publicity seeker, but rather preferred the friendly camaraderie of his colleagues and was greatly relieved when some of this adulation finally wore off.

However, on the track he was something of a showman. Because of his complete confidence and relaxed attitude, he was fully at ease in competition, apparently quite oblivious that he was the center of attraction. His zest for running added to his popularity and his extra lap of honor following a victory became famous. As he would circle the track smiling broadly and acknowledging the crowd's satisfaction, the spectators would roar their approval of his gracious manner. Kip's running suit was evidence of a policeman's pride in his personal appearance. The bright green shirt contrasted with his spotless white running trunks and were usually topped off by a brilliantly colored orange cap. The cap-souvenir from Tokyo's Olympics would invariable be flung high in the air as he unleashed his powerful final kick to grind his opponents into the cinders. The crowd would cheer him on to victory following this dramatic gesture.

At home on his farm at Kapchemoiywo, Kip is again the shy, retiring husband and father of four daughters—a genuine family man. He likes nothing better than to journey 250 miles from his police station to the peaceful rural life of his twenty-two-acre farm and to revel in the company of his family. Jane, a sweet, efficient homemaker, operates the farm in Kip's absence and maintains high Christian standards in the raising of her children. On the farm Kip enjoys the simple Nandi diet of "murzic"—a thick curdled cow's milk that is often stewed for weeks in a calabash, and "ugali"—the thick cereal mush—plus green vegetables, game meat, and fresh fruit. He does not smoke or touch any form of alcohol, and frequently urges young athletes to abstain from these debilitating habits.

Kip's Christian testimony is well known in Kenya, where he is an elder of the African Inland Church of Nairobi. Very practical in his faith, he was urged at the height of his career by his aged father to give up running because of the fear of witchcraft. The old man worried about jealous competitors who might try to bewitch or poison his son. "Nonsense," replied Keino, "God is there to protect and guide me, and He is stronger than the evil spirits." The father, not yet a Christian believer, continues to ponder his son's answer. Meanwhile he keeps informed daily about Kip's safety when he runs overseas, still dubious about the power of God over the evil spirits. Countless thousands of Africans still living in fear have been impressed by Kip's faith in the living God and have heard him witness to the only solution to that fear—personal faith in Jesus Christ.

Through the months that followed his record runs, invitations from around the world took Keino into nearly every international track meet. He became more and more attracted to the world's best-known race, the mile, and its metric equivalent, the 1,500-meters. Finally he decided to run that distance as well as his classic 5,000- and 10,000-meter races, and began rigorous training for the three events in the Mexico Olympics.

With confidence and high hopes, he arrived in Mexico City after a grueling training session at 7,000 feet altitude in the mountains of Kenya. Prospects for victory looked pretty dim, however, following Keino's collapse on the track during the 10,000-meter race. A West German doctor diagnosed his difficulty as a gall bladder infection, casting doubt on his ability to compete in the tough 1,500-meter event. But the determined Kenyan decided to run as long as he had breath.

After the semifinals in which both Kip and his young understudy Ben Jipcho qualified, the team met for a strategy session. The Kenyan officials had been told by the doctor that an operation might be necessary and that Kip should be hospitalized for observation and X ray. With characteristic determination, Keino said without hesitation, that he would rather die on the track running for his country than on a hospital bed. Immediately he began to talk about race tactics. Most of the team didn't believe in his present condition he could out-kick world record holder Jim Ryun at the end of the race. The American had shown excellent form in the preliminary heats, and everyone predicted he would repeat his previous victories over Keino, even at Mexico's high altitude. That is, everyone was doubtful that he could win except Keino himself and his young understudy—the two Kenyans still in the race!

Ben Jipcho was the key man. He was a very promising miler, who had qualified for the finals with a better time than his friend Kip. More important, he was a Christian colleague who loved Keino as his own brother. He knew that in a fast race Kip could still win. And he was determined to see that it *was* a fast race, even if it meant sacrificing his own chance to win a medal. Instead of planning his race for a victory, Jipcho planned to set a fast first-half pace for Keino that would give him enough lead to carry him to victory.

Race time came. Young Jipcho shot into the lead of the 1,500-meter finals from the opening gun with Kip close behind. He maintained his blistering pace, knowing that he was running himself out. He reached the halfway mark in an amazing 1:53.3. Here Kip sprinted wide and took the lead from his pace-setter as Ryun moved up from ninth, preparing for his famous fast finish. But Kip was still sprinting and before Ryun knew it, he found himself 40 yards behind. Jim broke into his well-known sprint, overtook one man, and headed for Kip; but it was too late; Keino hit the finish line 20 yards ahead of Ryun in a stunning upset. As Kip won his gold medal for Kenya, he threw his hands into the air in the typical Keino salute to the crowd. This time it was much more than a sporting gesture, it was thanks to God for many things—among them a self-sacrificing brother in Christ, Ben Jipcho, whose pace-setting early in the race had made possible his victory.

Four years later, in the 1972 terror laden summer games in Munich, Germany, Keino and Jipcho teamed up again for one of the most outstanding upsets ever. Having run the 3,000-meter steeplechase just three times previously, Keino took the lead with less than a third of the race to go. He looked anything but graceful as he doggedly charged over the barriers in the unconventional gait of a nonexperienced steeplechaser.

Jipcho, with a little more finesse, hung with him much of the way. At the finish, it was Keino and Jipcho for the gold and silver and a new world's record. Clearly, Keino had established himself as the world's premier stamina man. While he may never break the world record in the mile run, his fierce determination and his ability to call on seemingly inexhaustible reserves of strength make him a threat at any distance and virtually unbeatable in the steeplechase.

In the 1,500 meters at Munich, world mile record-holder Jim Ryun of the United States was eliminated in the semifinals in a bad spill, and suddenly the final race appeared anticlimactic. Characteristically, Keino was the first to try to console the stunned American, but the long awaited showdown between the best and the defending gold medalist was now an impossibility. Some say that competitive edge was now lost to Keino; others speculate that the grueling steeplechase took too much out of him. But Kip would be the first to admit that he was simply outrun by Finland's top metric miler. The Finns took the gold in the 1,500, the 5,000, and the 10,000.

Keino was disappointed, but Kenya more than settled for a silver medal in the event.

That day in the hotel at Bouaké, Ivory Coast, my attention went from one to the other of these two men who made such a great team on the track. Not only did Kip Keino share his personal faith in Christ, but Ben Jipcho told of his Christian training in an American Church of God school. I asked Kip what counsel he would give to young people desirous of running. He quickly summarized it in two words. "Work hard!" Then he added, "To be successful in anything requires a determination to keep fit and to win. I attribute any success I have had to dependence on God, constant training, and a lot of courage."

"And what would you say to young people in order to make their lives count for Christ?" I asked.

"God gave me the gift of athletic ability," he replied, "and He has given each Christian specific gifts. Just as it is my job to cultivate my gift by rigorous training and personal discipline, so Christian young people should develop their individual gifts and each exercise his own for God's glory."

10
I Preach Christ as the Black Man's Hope

by TOM SKINNER

as told to James R. Adair

Seventeen years ago I led gang wars for one of New York City's most notorious black teen gangs, the Lords. Today I am telling my people that faith in Jesus Christ—not violence—is our only hope. There are a handful of other young blacks like myself in the United States. Most of us are in our twenties and thirties. I suppose you could say in a sense we are the "black hope," for today in many areas a growing number of blacks are branding Bible-based preaching as the "white man's religion." We believe God has called us to Himself so that we can share with blacks the great truth that His plan of salvation is for all—black or white.

It isn't always easy, or physically safe.

At a mass meeting in front of the Theresa Hotel in Harlem several years ago I said that some of the blame for the problems in the Harlem community had to be placed on the "white power structure." But I also pointed out that there are certain things that can't be blamed on white people.

"The white man isn't standing over us with a knife making sixty thousand of us become drug addicts. Neither is he causing ten thousand illegitimate children to be born in our community. And he isn't causing 126 million dollars of liquor to be consumed every year—just in Harlem," I said.

I did my best to show them that these problems resulted from sin in the human heart—in the hearts of blacks. When sixty-five or seventy people stepped out of the crowd, indicating their desire to receive Jesus Christ and let Him rule their lives, black nationalist leaders circulated through the crowd shouting, "Lynch him! Lynch him!"

At another time when seventeen responded to the invitation to let Christ take over their lives, a semicircle of Black Muslims approached me after the meeting.

"You preach the white man's religion," their leader said.

"I'm not preaching anybody's religion—I'm preaching God," I replied.

They moved in menacingly. Suddenly a man burst through the crowd. He pulled open his shirt to show a knife scar across his chest.

"Tom Skinner did this to me six years ago. He's different now, man. What he says is true. God can change the meanest man—he changed Tom."

The men stopped. Then they quietly walked away. The friend who came to my rescue was one of my old gang cohorts. He and I once fought for gang leadership, and I had slashed him across the chest. A month after he came to my defense I learned that he was found stabbed to death.

Over in Cleveland sometime later I was accosted by a gang of toughs, who tossed the same "white religion" insults at me.

"You fight?" one fellow challenged.

"Would you if I would?" I asked. God has given me pretty good equipment (6 feet tall, 210 pounds) and I hadn't exactly forgotten how.

"Yeah, man."

"Okay. And if I beat you—you come to the meeting?"

The tough backed off. He continued to heckle, but I shouted him down and told him that Jesus Christ was the only remedy for his condition. Later in a meeting, this same fellow with other members of his family came forward in response to the invitation.

Not many years ago I was a rebel and hated Christianity myself. Maybe that's why they listen to me. I grew up in the shadows of the old Polo Grounds smack in the middle of Harlem. My dad was a preacher, but I became a rebel. When I was twelve, a fellow invited me to become a member of the notorious Harlem Lords. That evening he introduced me to the leaders, and to the rest of the gang. They gave me three choices for initiation: (1) hang by my wrists from a spike on a brick wall, and take twenty lashes without making a noise; (2) three guys would beat me senseless; (3) my face would be turned to the wall, and a blindfolded guy would walk fifteen paces away and turn and hurl a knife; if he missed, I was a member of the gang. I took the choice of being whipped.

After several months as gang member, I said to myself, "Why should I just be a member of the gang—why not the leader?" This meant I had to challenge the present leader and beat him in front of the gang. There were three choices for fighting: (1) with bare fists; (2) with sticks, using garbage pail lids as shields; or (3) with knives. Well, I beat the leader by using my fists. Soon after that

I was challenged by two other fellows and beat them. For the next two years I was leader of the Lords.

During those years I led a double life. Most gang leaders are dropouts or school problems. As a student at Junior High School 139, I made good grades. I was a member of the Arista Society, secretary of the debate team, president of the Shakespearean Club. At church I was president of the young people's department, sang in the young people's choir, and led Bible discussions. But rumbling with the gang was my big interest.

Occasionally I ordered gang members to chase me home. I would run into the house out of breath to make my folks think I was being chased by the bad guys. In those days I led the fellows in fifteen gang fights, all of which we won. I studied history and picked up ancient military and modern military tactics that I applied to fighting on the streets —tactics from Greek and Roman battles, like surprising the enemy by making them think our numbers were few, and then sending fellows in hiding swooping down on them.

Right in the middle of this mess God spoke to me. The evening of October 12, 1956, I was planning strategy for a gang fight to out-rumble all gang fights. It would involve about three thousand fellows. I had my radio on, listening to my favorite rock 'n' roll program. At 9:00 P.M. an unscheduled gospel program came on. I almost turned the dial to another station but, somehow, though I was sick and tired of religion, I listened.

To this day I do not know the name of the evangelist. His poor grammar jarred me, but his message spoke to my heart. He spoke on II Corinthians 5:17, "If any man be in Christ, he is a new creature. . . ." I became convicted of my sins, and simply took Christ at His word: "Him that cometh to me, I will in no wise cast out."

"If that's true, I'm coming," I said. And that's when God took over my life.

Now I knew I had to quit the gang. Two weeks before, I had broken the arms and a leg of another fellow who tried to quit. (The procedure to break his arms was simple: we laid him flat on his belly with his arms behind his back; then I jumped on him, snapping his arms.)

What would happen to me when I announced I was quitting? I couldn't help but think about it; yet somehow I believed God would see me through. One of the Scriptures the radio evangelist quoted was, "Lo, I am with you always, even unto the end of the world." Another that was helpful was, "He which hath begun a good work in you will perform it until the day of Jesus Christ."

The following night I told the fellows I was through. At first they thought I was joking. They realized I was serious when I walked away. Two nights later The Mop, our number two man, cornered me. (We called him The Mop because in a gang war he always drew blood and ceremoniously mopped his foot in it.)

"Tom, I want to talk to you. The other night I was going to come at you with my knife and get you in the back. But the funniest thing happened: I couldn't move. Something glued me to that seat," he said.

Then I knew that the Lord was practical. He had not only saved me spiritually, but He was demonstrating His power to keep me in my life. That night The Mop became my first convert to Jesus Christ. He got out of the gang in much the way I did, and has gone on to identify himself with Christ. Several years ago he graduated from

Columbia Law School. Two other gang members later made decisions for Christ.

A further indication of God's grace at work in my heart and life occurred in a football game a few weeks after my conversion. As a guard, I pulled out to block for a halfback and crashed into a defensive end, the ball carrier going over for a touchdown. The man I had blocked, a white boy, slammed a fist into my stomach and then cracked me on the back of the neck. Under former conditions I would have tangled with him. But by the grace of God I was able to get up and smile and say something like, "You know, despite what you just did to me, I love you in the name of Jesus Christ."

Today, after four years' study at Manhattan Bible Institute and two years at Wagner College, I find God still demonstrating His love and power as the Holy Spirit shows me how to talk about Himself to my people in Harlem and other areas.

In past summers especially I have tried to mix with the people in Harlem. I join a group of fellows at a playground and play basketball with them, or swim with them at Colonial pool at 145th and Bradhurst, and over a period of days get to know them. At first I don't mention God or religion. Finally I find out the leader and get better acquainted with him, taking him perhaps to see sights outside his neighborhood. I tell him a bit about my background and the fact that I too was one time a gang leader. "Want to know how I got out? Well, I'll tell you. . . ." And at this point I begin to introduce him to Jesus Christ. God has given me more than a dozen young fellows through situations like this—leaders of such gangs as the Diablos, the Imperials, the Crowns, the Sportsmen.

I've been in homes where there are seven or eight children who have as many as three or four fathers. I eat with such families by the light of a 75-watt bare bulb hanging from the ceiling. Cockroaches crawl on the walls, mice and rats run across the floor. These are my people. My job is to share with them the wonderful news of the man Jesus Christ, and show them how He can be relevant in their lives.

God has also given me opportunities to help them through a radio ministry and in mass meetings. In recent years God has drawn many to Himself in campaigns in such cities as Chicago, Boston, Philadelphia, Cleveland, Grand Rapids, Detroit, as well as New York. [Tom Skinner crusades are conducted under the auspices of Tom Skinner Associates, Inc., Box C, Brooklyn, N.Y. 11202.]

My strategy is not to limit those to whom I preach. But I have to be realistic enough to know that in spite of the civil rights movement (or because of it—depending on your point of view) fewer and fewer white evangelists are willing to pay the price necessary to win people of my race. And with so few black evangelicals preaching a clear-cut gospel message, there is a desperate need.

Some white people don't realize that many blacks lag behind their white counterparts in certain areas of life. Why do blacks have a limited concept of family life, morals, economic security, the political structure, and the authority of the police? Unless you understand this, you will never get through to the blacks in order to help them.

Take, for example, the image of the father in the family. In white circles he is the picture of authority, of strength. Not so among most of the black population.

"I have two hundred kids coming to my youth activity who are living separated, Christ-centered lives . . . but only five of them have fathers to whom they can turn for help and advice. I have to be father to all the rest," a worker with black young people in a Midwest city recently told me.

The reason for this situation is both historic and economic. In slave days there was no such thing as family life among most of the slaves. They were mated according to the whims of the slave owner who wanted healthy offspring. All decisions were made for the black slave, so there was no opportunity for the father to assert his position as head of a house.

Today social workers find themselves stymied time and time again because of the results of this background, particularly because economic conditions today have reemphasized the problem.

Most blacks in our large Northern cities have moved up from the South. Lack of education kept them from getting well-paying jobs. The sons in the family became school dropouts in order to take the economic load off the family. The girls continue through high school. As a result they are able to get lucrative secretarial jobs that provide a better salary than the male without high school education can get. The result? The person who "brings home the bacon" makes the decisions in the family. Is it any wonder so many husbands simply disappear?

As we have seen in Harlem and elsewhere, black believers themselves are most effective in making Christ relevant to the black man. In our work, we must win them to ourselves first, and then to Christ. We are careful not to use stereotyped religious phrases; we use the language of the street.

You have to be direct. It gets through better if I say, "You know, man, you know what the Bible says about you? You stink! That's right. In God's sight you smell. Jesus Christ wants to clean up your life and make you a new person." That gets to them. They listen.

I try to show my people that Jesus Christ is interested in their problems. They are talking about police brutality, prejudice, economic development, black bourgeoisie, black business, economic advancement, integration. I tell them that to bring about the changes they want to see in their society, a change has to come in the hearts of those who make up that society.

The Black Muslim would bring about a black reformation. The black nationalist wants to drive out white businessmen and establish black business. Don't think for a minute that the Muslims are bums; they are a well-disciplined bunch, clean fellows–never drunk, never out of work. The nationalists are not as high class. They are more violent than the Muslims.

But even these people are not unreachable. In a crusade in Harlem, among the first converts to respond to the invitation were two Black Muslims. I remember dealing with a young Black Muslim after a street meeting at 116th Street and Lenox Avenue in Harlem. I had spoken from the Scripture, "Look unto me, all the ends of the earth."

I had to break through the doctrinal barrier he set up. So we went to a restaurant for lunch. I couldn't speak merely in terms of a new life–he himself used the term *resurrected* in referring to my change. He could have told me of drug addicts or alcoholics who had shaken their habit, after joining the Black Muslims.

First I had to show him that King James had nothing to do with the message of the Bible, that the Bible went back to Greek and Hebrew manuscripts. Then we talked of Jesus Christ. One thing the Muslims will admit is that He was a perfect man. So I said, "If Jesus Christ was a perfect man, then it means that everything He said was perfect." The young man had to accept that. And once he did, he was cornered. From there on I just took what Jesus said about Himself, and that convinced him. That young man began walking with the Lord.

To reach the black of the twentieth century you have to understand him. You have to put yourself in his position so you can see things as he sees them. This is not so much lowering yourself to his level as it is recognizing his rights to the same things you enjoy. Once you have demonstrated that you understand him and recognize his God given rights, witnessing to him is no different from witnessing to anybody else.

In order to see blacks won to Christ, both black and white believers must come together at the foot of the cross of Christ and recognize their unity as members of the body of Christ. Once they have humbled themselves together, they can then rise in a program of evangelism which will not only result in black believers, but will enhance revival throughout the country.

I am not so naive as to think that because I have expressed my convictions, things are going to change overnight. And because I know this will take time, my plea now is for white believers to back those dedicated blacks who can take the gospel to their own people.

There are a number of young black evangelicals who are well trained, vitally interested in their own people, and moving ahead as best they can to reach them. Yet none of us is affluent; nor do we have support of larger organizations or foundations. Our effectiveness could be increased manifold if we had the prayers and financial assistance of white people and churches.

"Why don't black churches support these men

and others working for the blacks?" I am often asked. This is a good question. My answer is that we simply do not have the number of evangelical churches many people think we do. There are some, but relatively few in comparison to the many fly-by-night storefront operations of single individuals with a profiteering motive who are appealing to our inherent religious nature. The black is a person with a deep religious heritage in music and church membership. Yet relatively few blacks know Jesus Christ as personal Savior. The black person will support civil rights and other organizations striving to improve the lot of his race. But because he is not born again, he is not interested in the widespread proclamation of the gospel of Jesus Christ as the answer to blacks' problems.

Today young black evangelical leaders are already at work on the monumental task which lies in front of them. But they lack the tools to do a good job. These tools include support for a massive program of evangelism. Such a program would consist of tested methods of communication as gospel radio broadcasts and literature written specifically for the black. Happily, we have some writers if we can get the financial support for the publication of tracts, Bible correspondence courses, and booklets for new converts.

We need Christian education workshops in order to increase the black's ability to develop leaders for the local church. At least one publisher has proved the effectiveness of these. We also need a Christian magazine written for the black—a magazine which will increase communication among existing evangelical blacks and thus make evangelistic efforts easier.

Above all, the black evangelical today needs understanding and confidence from his white

Christian friends. Blacks are still hungry to know God—but we must work fast if we are to turn the tide of a growing antagonism toward what many blacks look on as the "white man's religion."

11
Jazz Was My Life

by HOWARD O. JONES

I could not believe my ears. Wanda, the one girl in all the world I wanted to marry, had refused me! Me, a rising young musician in a popular dance band, with a bright future ahead.

I promised Wanda fame and fortune, for I was sure that one day our dance band would be known from coast to coast as the jazz world's biggest and best dance orchestra. But Wanda was not swept off her feet with my ideas for our future together. She had other ideas—ideas that were very different from mine. And ideas that were new to her.

"Howard," she said, "even though I love you, I love Christ more. Therefore, unless you find Christ as your Savior, I must, for the sake of Christ, leave you because we have nothing in common."

What strange words! After all, I thought, I was just as religious as she was. Wasn't I a member of a church? Hadn't I been baptized? Wasn't that enough religion for one man? With Wanda, it was not enough.

The music of the jazz world had me in its grip. My musical career began in Cleveland, Ohio. I was born on April 12, 1921. My father was a lover of music and encouraged my brother and me to play a musical instrument for ourselves. I chose the clarinet; my brother chose the trumpet.

After about two years of hard practice, we were playing regularly in the church orchestra. Occasionally we played for other church programs and many secular affairs as well. My religious life was rather a nominal one, though each Sunday our whole family went to church together.

In the summer of 1934 my parents moved to the beautiful little college town of Oberlin, Ohio. My brother and I took our musical training seriously and enrolled for special training at the Oberlin Conservatory of Music.

While in my second year at Oberlin High School, I was invited to join a local dance band. My brother joined with me. My grandmother had already bought me a new saxophone, and before long I was the first saxophonist in this newly formed orchestra. Soon we were playing for dances and parties everywhere. I was thrilled, for I had always dreamed of being a great orchestra leader someday. I wanted nothing else in life.

But about this time a series of evangelistic meetings was held at my grandparents' church. One evening my brother and I and several friends attended the service. That night the evangelist preached a powerful sermon. He warned the congregation about sin and the need of getting right with God. Moved emotionally, I, along with my brother and the other fellows, went forward after the service.

As I knelt there that night, I felt that I should join the church and be baptized. I was sure if I did that, it would ensure me a place in heaven when I died. When we rose to our feet, the people with us began to shake our hands and rejoice that we had agreed to be baptized and become members of the church.

Finally came the Sunday night of the baptismal service. I waited eagerly for my turn. At last, my brother was immersed, and then I was. After we had come up out of the water, we hurried back to the dressing room, and changed our clothes. With our heads still wet we went out the back door of the church and into a waiting car and sped away to play for a big dance. But as we drove along, to my surprise a strange feeling of guilt overwhelmed me. I realized in my heart that what we were doing was wrong. With effort, I pushed the feeling aside and soon had lost myself in our discussion of the big dance.

The orchestra filled more and more important engagements. We were now in the public eye, and we delighted in the reports we got in the press.

One weekend our orchestra was away on one of our biggest engagements yet. While we were gone, my girlfriend, Wanda, attended a gospel service. During the meeting she took Christ as her Savior, saying she knew now she was saved from her sins. This was an answer to the prayers of her mother, who, before dying, had prayed for Wanda's salvation.

When I returned home from our band trip, eager to tell Wanda of the good time I had had, she would talk only of her new-found joy and peace in Christ Jesus.

"Howard," Wanda said, "the Lord has so completely forgiven me my sins and transformed my life that even my desires for worldly pleasures are all gone."

I was glad for Wanda's testimony of her faith. I told myself a little religion never hurt anyone. I had mine—and now she had hers. But it wasn't long before I found out that Wanda had something more than mere religion.

A few days after Wanda was saved, I asked her to go to the theater with me. She refused. This was most strange! Before her conversion, Wanda and I had always enjoyed the cinema very much—so I knew that something out of the ordinary must have happened. I asked Wanda to go dancing with me. Again she turned me down. This new Wanda amazed me. She was no longer interested in dancing or even in my work as a jazz musician.

Seeing Wanda's consistent Christian living and going to an evangelical church with her, I was confronted with the disturbing truth that there is a distinct difference between cold, ceremonial religion and a genuine born-again experience through personal faith in Christ Jesus.

I saw that being a baptized church member and choir singer did not assure me a place in heaven at all; and that unless I would repent of my many sins and believe fully in Christ, I would die unsaved and spend a Christless eternity in hell.

Before Wanda's conversion we had talked of getting married someday after high school graduation. But now she explained to me that unless I gave my heart to Christ, she would have to stop seeing me.

"Wanda," I begged her, "our differences of ideas on spiritual matters need not separate us. I love you, Wanda, and I'll be a great band leader someday, making lots of money. You'll never want for anything."

Then it was that I heard Wanda's fateful rejection.

Too stubborn and proud to give in, I told myself I could live without Wanda or her Savior. Our dance band, the fame, the popularity, the bright lights, and money—weren't these the things I wanted most? I tried to lose myself in my music and the social activity of the jazz world. But the more I tried, the more miserable I was in my mind and soul.

Worst of all, my unhappiness began to affect even my music. I couldn't play as I used to. All of a sudden I didn't enjoy jazz anymore. The wonderful, spine-tingling feeling that once thrilled me as we poured out the hot, swinging jazz rhythm was all gone now. I realized at last that I no longer played because I loved it—but because it was a job and the only work I knew how to do.

One Sunday night in my misery, as I sat in Wanda's church again, her pastor preached a sermon that God meant for me. I was so convicted of my sin by the Spirit of God that I went to the front and, on my knees, poured out my heart to God. I acknowledged my sinful condition to Him and begged His forgiving mercy for me, the poor, hell-bound sinner that I was.

That night God answered my prayer—and Wanda's prayer. He saved me. I stood up and testified that I was saved by faith in Christ. I was conscious that God had done something in me. I felt good in my heart. My mind was at rest. And for the first time in my life I knew that somewhere, somehow, God had something for me to do for Him.

From that night, things began to happen. I threw away my cigarettes and gave up my smoking. I never drank again. I stopped going to the cinema. Even dancing became a thing of the past for me. But one great battle remained to be fought between me and the Lord. God made it clear to me that as a born-again Christian, I must leave the dance band forever and surrender my life fully to Him.

But now that I was a Christian, I still hoped

secretly that I could love Christ, Wanda, and my jazz. I knew in my heart I was wrong, but I fought the Lord for it anyway. God was putting His hand on the very idol of my life—the orchestra.

One of the country's most famous orchestras was coming to town to play for a dance at a popular nightclub on the lakeshore. All the old gang of friends I had known were going. If ever I felt the power of Satan tempting me to go to a dance, it was then. I had no doubt that God was against it, and I knew what Wanda thought about it, but she was away visiting relatives in another city.

I decided on what I thought would be a good solution—a compromise. I would go to the dance, but only to drive my brother and his girl friend there. When we arrived at the big park, I stayed around outside the ballroom talking with my old friends. Soon someone asked about my acceptance of Christ. It seemed that nearly everyone there had heard of my trip to the church front to find salvation.

"Howard, now that you are a Christian, are you going to leave the band?" one asked.

"Yes," I said. "I do feel that God wants me to leave the band. At times I even feel as though God wants me to preach the gospel. But as to when I am going to leave the band, I am not prepared to say right now."

Later I began to reason with myself: perhaps it wouldn't be a sin if I just went in and listened to the music—as long as I kept my promise not to do any dancing.

As I argued with myself, I moved closer and closer to the door of the big hall. When I got inside, I did not experience the secret thrill I had hoped for. Beads of perspiration stood out on my forehead. My heart pounded as though I had just run a race. I began trembling all over. Some of our band members noticed me. "Howard, are you sick?" one asked.

"No, I'm not sick," I answered. "I'll be all right in a minute."

I started to panic. "I've got to get out of here—fast!" I told myself. Turning quickly, I walked as fast as I could to the nearest exit. The clean, cool night air swept over me. Tears of shame streamed down my face as I looked up into the beautiful star-lit sky and cried out to God from the depths of my soul.

"O God!" I cried, "if You will forgive my sins this night, and my disobedience, I will serve You the rest of my life. Lord, I know that You want me to leave the band and surrender my life to You. Tonight, Lord, if You will help me, I will leave the orchestra and accept Your call to preach the gospel of Christ."

God heard my prayer. He answered it by lifting the heavy weight of conviction and guilt. And then He flooded my soul with peace and joy such as I had never known before.

After I left the band, I really began to live for Christ; but along with my new life and joy came trouble, too. Playing long hours for dances and running day and night with the old high-life gang had broken my health. I suffered strange fainting spells and serious attacks of indigestion.

Finally I went to a doctor. He said my blood pressure was that of a person sixty-five years old. As if that was not enough, the doctor warned me that my condition was so serious that even if I did live to be thirty years old, I would be a complete physical wreck. My indigestion was caused by nervous disorders. Then began a long period of rest, diet, and medical treatment for my recovery.

One evening an attack of indigestion was so painful that I could do nothing but go to bed. As

I lay there in agony, I began to pray to God. I told the Lord that I knew I was saved, but I still was not sure if He really wanted me to preach the gospel. I was willing, but I did not see how I could serve Him with such a sick body. I asked Him to heal my body and deliver me from my misery so that I might serve Him well.

After praying I fell into a deep sleep. As I slept the Lord gave me an amazing vision. I saw myself standing by the pulpit of a very large church. With arms outstretched I invited the people to come to Christ. God was there in our midst as men and women found Christ as their Savior.

It was morning when I awoke. To my amazement, as I got out of bed I felt wonderful. Then and there I knew that God had called me to preach the gospel and that He would completely heal my sick body. In time, He did just that.

Then came the big day in June 1941 when Wanda and I together graduated from Oberlin High School. Three months later we both entered the Missionary Training Institute in Nyack, New York, where we began preparing for Christian service together. In June 1944 we were graduated from the Institute and were married.

In January 1952, after eight busy years of preaching in New York, I was called to Cleveland, Ohio, as pastor of the Christian and Missionary Alliance Smoot Memorial Church. And here, as well, God saved many souls.

In October 1958, God led me to my present assignment as an associate evangelist with the Billy Graham Evangelistic Association. My work has taken me to many parts of the world, including Africa, to preach the glorious gospel of Christ and invite men and women of all races and colors to come to the Savior to receive forgiveness and new life.

Little did I realize that when I gave my life to Christ that night long ago, He would use me in the way that He has. To me it is proof of God's love and mercy. If He can use me, He can use anyone.

12 He Helps Seaway Succeed

by BILL KRUTZA

The spotlight has fallen on Seaway National Bank because it is one of two Chicago banks that has an integrated staff and ownership with blacks in predominance. Situated in an integrated area on Chicago's South Side, Seaway employs people from various ethnic backgrounds who have come together to work in harmony and contribute substantially to a highly successful organization.

A lion's share of the credit goes to Richard Linyard, Seaway's executive vice-president, the man who put the staff together when the bank was opened in 1965.

"Presently we have about forty black workers and twenty whites. We've proved that integration works," he says. "We have very wholesome and challenging relationships. All employees are judged on their abilities and desires to work in the organization."

Linyard directs all hiring and employee relations practices. Beyond this are his responsibilities for the complete operational functions, seeing that the bank is properly insured, and seeing that all assets are fully protected.

Linyard's friendly, yet straightforward, contacts with employees about working conditions, promotions, and other aspects of their jobs often inspire employees to ask him for advice on strictly personal matters.

Recently an employee came to him with a family problem. She and her husband were on the verge of separation. In the course of the conversation, Linyard suggested that he and the woman pray. He closed the draperies to shut them off from the busyness of the bank and committed her problem to the Lord. Then he covenanted with her to pray daily at 6:00 A.M. for the situation. She also promised to pray at that time. Within a few weeks the marriage was a happy, working relationship.

Customers also come into Linyard's office—usually to solve financial problems. In discussing money matters with them, Linyard often discovers far deeper problems—those of a personal nature. Often the personal problems brought on the financial crises.

While the customer pours out his story of personal woes, Linyard seeks to recall a Bible passage appropriate for the distraught person. He often quotes the passage he believes has meant more than any other in his personal experience: Proverbs 3:5, 6—"Trust in the Lord with all thine heart; and lean not unto thine own understanding. In all thy ways acknowledge him, and he shall direct thy paths."

"When the personal problem is solved," Linyard says, "it's much simpler to solve the business problems of an individual."

Because he has to make decisions that affect the lives of many people and also the future operations of the bank, he says, "I have to ask the Lord for wisdom to accomplish my tasks. As far as I'm concerned, without daily guidance from Him, I could not fulfill my responsibilities."

Linyard developed this attitude of dependence on the Lord in earlier years. As a boy he often listened to his father pray. His father spent a considerable amount of time away from home as a chauffeur for an industrialist. When he returned home, Richard, along with his eight brothers and sisters, listened carefully to the exciting stories he would tell and also to his wise spiritual counsel. This godly influence, Richard says, made a great impact on his life.

During high school days in Maywood, Illinois, Richard also developed another good attitude toward life—ambition! Much of this came through his vigorous participation in sports. As a lanky six-footer, he did well on the Proviso High School track teams. His high jump record stood for sixteen years after his graduation. Even now he maintains a slimmed-down weight through active participation at the local YMCA's paddle ball court.

His interest in banking started while he worked in a clothing store after school and on Saturdays. The clothing store was situated across the street from the Oak Park Trust and Savings Bank. Regularly he went into the bank to purchase money orders. The cashier often noticed him and one day asked Richard, "Would you like to work here?"

That was in 1950. For the next five years, Richard worked as janitor at the bank. Next he became the elevator operator. From there he was promoted to work as savings department bookkeeper, then to savings teller, then to general bookkeeper, then to superintendent of the bookkeeping department, then to assistant manager of the savings department, and finally to the job of assistant cashier.

Linyard came to Seaway National as cashier in December 1964 to help organize the bank and hire its fully integrated staff before the bank opened a month later. In June 1965 he was elected to his present position.

"Every day is an exciting experience," he proclaims. "No two days are the same. I never know when I answer one of my two almost constantly ringing phones what the challenge may be—either to solve an immediate situation or to enter into some long-range plans or to go on a trip as one of the directors of the Chicago chapter of the American Institute of Banking."

To keep mentally and spiritually alert for each day, Linyard gets up early enough to have a time of quiet meditation. During this time he consciously commits the day to the Lord and seeks some instruction from the Bible. He knows that as soon as the bank doors open, he'll have little or no time for meditation. Without this early morning preparation, he says he would be unprepared to face what he simply labels "the rat race."

Those moments alone with Christ supply the energy and wisdom his banking day demands. With confidence in the leading of the Lord, he launches into his tasks of counseling people concerning what to do with their money—advising some concerning wise borrowing habits, advising others to make good investments; settling any problems that arise in personal relationships or in operational procedures; taking advantage of opportunities to point people to the divine Problem Solver.

"I find that if I don't take out this time in the early morning before I work, things don't go as smoothly as they should," he says. "But when

Christ in is control, mountains become foothills and the love of Christ directs my thinking and actions."

When asked if he has any ambitions, Linyard said nothing about promotions in the banking world. He simply and humbly said, "I want to find myself so wrapped up in Christ that if someone looks at me, they will see Christ shining through my life in everything I do either here at Seaway National, or in my church life, or in my home."

With such an attitude conveyed to the employees at Seaway, it's no wonder that there are good relationships between the blacks and whites who work there!

13
Canary Brown Sings Out for God

by HELEN F. GOODMAN

You would have thought the Pied Piper had reappeared. Children dashed out of their ghetto homes and down the sidewalk, all headed in the same direction. Had you joined the exodus and asked what it was all about, you might have heard a breathless, "Going to a party!" or "It's a party at Mrs. Brown's house!"

Soon, over one hundred children gathered in front of a house that seemed to stand out from all the others. It was the one house with good paint, flowers and shrubs in the yard, and crisp curtains at the windows. There, seated on improvised benches in front of Mrs. Canary Brown's Lansing, Michigan, home, the happy gang eagerly devoured sloppy-joes, potato chips, Kool-Aid–and a Bible story.

The Bible story was the real reason for the party, for Canary Brown's one aim in life is to "tell them about Jesus, 'cause knowing Him is so wonderful!" Past the half-century mark, and battling a chronic physical ailment, Canary serves as part-time volunteer secretary at Family Life Radio, a Christian station in Lansing, and does part-time domestic work to earn a living. The hours she spends in serving the Lord, however, make her a full-time missionary.

Once a week children crowd into her tiny living room for an hour of Bible study in her Good News Club. Many are from broken homes, or have alcoholic parents, and have no spiritual help at home. Canary gives them the gospel with each lesson and also teaches them how to study the Bible for themselves.

Early one evening Canary's phone rang. A childish voice piped, "Mrs. Brown, can you come over and talk to my daddy? My brother asked him a Bible question, and he doesn't know the answer. I told him *you* could answer it."

"I'll be right over," promised Canary, recognizing the caller as a girl who had recently accepted Jesus as her Savior in Good News Club.

Canary talked with the parents and found their Bible knowledge pitifully meager, but they had a desire to learn. She offered to meet with them weekly to study the Bible. This study group has grown to include several other adults of the neighborhood.

Mrs. Brown delights in serving the Lord in hard places. Going to the pastor of a church in her neighborhood, she asked permission to have a vacation Bible school in his church.

"You're welcome to try," he replied, "but you won't get over fifteen to come. The kids around here just won't go to church!"

Canary contacted her prayer partner and together they asked the Lord for forty children to come to VBS the next morning.

When the pastor arrived to unlock the doors,

there were already forty-two excited youngsters waiting to get into his church. The total enrollment that week was seventy-nine, and several trusted Jesus Christ as their personal Savior as a direct result.

Mrs. Brown is also a volunteer counselor with the probate court, meeting weekly with a group of eight to ten delinquent teen-agers.

Not long ago she wanted to take her group of teens to see the Christian film "For Pete's Sake." However, her supervisor denied permission. Determined that these young people should see the film, Canary went to the next person in charge. The answer was the same. Three more times she tried and finally was told that if another person was with her she could take them.

"There is another Person with me," Mrs. Brown said, beaming. "You don't see Him, but Jesus is with me!" Permission was granted. Her persistence paid off, for one of the boys trusted Christ as his Savior that evening.

Canary Brown even goes to camp. As a volunteer counselor at Youth Haven, a camp for underprivileged children in Rives Junction, Michigan, she teaches Scripture verses to children who may never have seen a Bible before.

Canary's ambition to become a missionary began when she was just a child, even before she understood what Christianity was. She was taken to Sunday school and church regularly by her grandmother, but "never heard the gospel once in that little Arkansas Sunday school." However, she felt a deep love for God, and wanted to tell others about Him. She would line up chairs, place sticks on them for people, and teach her imaginary class.

Canary's parents had both died by the time she was ten. Her grandmother cared for her about three years; then she too died. The grandmother had been housekeeper for a Jewish doctor. Since there were no relatives to take Canary, the doctor took her into his family.

Canary was about fourteen when she walked into a settlement on the outskirts of Little Rock, Arkansas, one day and saw a woman telling a Bible story to a group of children on the street. She stopped and listened, fascinated by the kindness of the lady's face. Her story ended, the lady turned to Canary, "Are you a born-again believer?" she inquired.

"I don't know what that is," replied Canary, "but I do know I want to be a missionary and tell people about God."

Carefully the woman explained that one must be a Christian first to be a real missionary. Using John 3:16, she explained the love of God that sent His Son to save the world. Though it was the first time Canary had ever heard that Jesus Christ died for her sins, she trusted Him that day as her Savior.

With her conversion came a longing to study the Bible, but she could find no one to help her. Her limited education and reading ability made it difficult to study much on her own.

At age sixteen Canary married George Brown, but after only three years he died. Canary moved to Chicago. There she lived and worked for twenty years and never met anyone who, to her knowledge, was a Christian.

"I went to church," says Canary, "but no one carried a Bible, not even the pastor."

It wasn't until Canary and her small adopted son, LeRoy, had moved to Michigan that she finally found a church where the Bible was taught: the Inter-City Bible Church of Lansing. While in Chicago she had learned to read fairly well. Now, for the first time in her life, she really began to study Scripture.

Her first opportunity for serving the Lord came when she began teaching a Child Evangelism class.

"Oh, how I had to study in order to teach those children," Mrs. Brown recalls, "but it was just what I needed. I learned right along with them."

Soon she was teaching several classes among black children in Van Buren county.

In spite of her limited education, Canary determined to work for the Lord all she could; and she has found there is no lack of work to do for Him. She even began adult education courses and has now obtained her high school diploma.

Her ready smile and her oft repeated, "Praise the Lord!" conceal the fact there is pain in her life—physical pain from a chronic illness and an aching heart because of her son who is away from the Lord.

Friends have urged her to slow up, take more time for herself, get some rest, but Canary Brown's reaction is, "There were so many years I didn't know how to serve the Lord. Now I feel I must use every minute to work for Him!"

14
I'll Never Forget Joseph

by MARIAN POND

Albarka mu ba! "Thank You, my Father."

The rhythmic rattling of buckets accompanied by hearty ejaculations of praise broke the early morning stillness. Joseph strode down the path past our house to the well. All was quiet for a moment and then he prayed. Every word came through clear as a bell. A little later he came past our window again with full buckets, full voice, and full heart.

Joseph Ambapilu is an unforgettable African Christian who, more than anyone I have ever known, literally lives the words, "Rejoice evermore. Pray without ceasing. In everything give thanks."

Joseph, a farmer, left his hometown of Sardine in the northern part of the Mali Republic, West Africa, to attend the two-month laymen's Bible school course at our mission station of Sangha in Dogon tribe territory in Mali.

His pastor had told us about him. "Joseph is an unusual Christian," he said, "but studying is hard for him. His gift is faith. He prays all the time, everywhere, about everything."

The next few months proved the truth of those words.

Joseph is the tallest African I have ever seen. Well over six feet, his lanky frame is covered by homespun baggy trousers hanging in tatters at the knees and a badly frayed old suit coat. His huge feet are bare. A homespun cap set at a rakish angle tops off the outfit. Minus one eye and quite knock-kneed, he is far from being handsome. Yet his face has such a kind expression that one is immediately drawn to him.

Joseph turned from fetishism to God several years ago. Later he backslid and became a Muslim. After a few months, intense conviction brought him back to church. He confessed his sin and God completely changed him. From that day he has lived strictly for Christ. He witnesses to one after another and is always seeking opportunities to help others. With the indwelling of the Holy Spirit came the spirit of joy.

When school opened I soon discovered that Joseph has a voice commensurate with his height. In the evening prayer service his fervent *aleluya* almost lifted me right off the bench. A crying baby was no hindrance at all when he testified.

After prayer service everyone went home to bed —everyone except Joseph, that is. He went into the classroom nearest our house and continued praying. His praying, singing, and praising was all mixed up. Praying along, he sometimes would leave a sentence dangling while he burst into song. Praise, prayer, song—it was all one to him. Finally he slept. But when the roosters began crowing Joseph again began praying and singing.

Daybreak found him on the path to the well—singing. One song was his favorite, "Come to Jesus,

He Is Our Savior." It has ten verses and he delighted in singing it through several times.

Back from the well he struggled with syllables until class time. True, reading was hard for him. But he worked at it diligently.

Recess time: Joseph prayed out by a big rock.

Noon: He prayed in the garden.

Work time: He was given the job of watering the trees, which he did as he communed aloud with the Lord.

Six o'clock: Back from the well with two buckets of water and a heart bursting with praise.

He usually read from 6:00 P.M. until dark. Persistence and patience paid off. He was thrilled the day he came to show us his newly acquired New Testament.

After school was over, his pastor advised Joseph to stay and work on his reading a while longer. Our missionary neighbors, whose house is near ours, left on a trip. The house was placed in Joseph's care. He slept on the back porch—the nearest part of the house to our bedroom windows! Every night he followed his regular pattern of prayer and praise.

One day Joseph said someone had suggested to him that maybe it wasn't necessary to pray and sing at night like that. But the silence just didn't seem right. The next night he was back on schedule! "It was like being in prison," he said.

Joseph was greatly burdened for his family, none of whom were Christians. Perhaps the hardest thing he has had to take from them was their sneer: "You've left the fetish; you'll never get a wife."

In this country a man who has lost an eye has a difficult time finding a wife; it was no idle threat. Joseph simply made this a matter of prayer.

Joseph's prayer has been answered. For years he

had endured the taunts of his family and townspeople, "You're a one-eyed Christian; you'll never get a wife." Since his initial committal to God he prayed diligently about this and rested quietly awaiting God's will. Eventually an answer came: a young Christian widow was glad to become a one-eyed farmer's wife.

According to Dogon custom, all the members of a family work together in their fields and share the harvest. It has been difficult for Joseph since his conversion because of his father's opposition. Last year, before the farming season, the father cut him off from the rest of the family. Neighbors told the father he would be sorry because God is with Joseph. But the father was adamant.

Serene in the peace Jesus gives, Joseph slashed out a new field and planted alone. He harvested more than the combined efforts that all the rest of his family could produce.

One day Joseph was working in his field alone when he was bitten by a deadly viper. He immediately knelt in prayer, then got up and walked home. He asked his pastor's wife for some antiseptic powder. She asked him why he wanted it and he simply replied, "I know why I need it." She gave him a little which he took with him to the church.

Pressing it into the fang marks, he again knelt in prayer—and remained in prayer all night. Naturally speaking, he should have gotten desperately ill and died, perhaps by morning. But the sun arose and Joseph walked out of the church, the foot only slightly swollen. Several days later he shared what had happened with his fellow Christians.

Amazed, they demanded, "Why didn't you tell us?"

"I didn't want to cause you concern," replied Joseph. Persevering prayer combined with implicit faith in God, in my opinion, brought him through a situation that would have killed most men.

Joseph now serves the Lord as a layman in his village of Sardine. He and his wife constantly and consistently witness to the reality of faith in Jesus Christ.

Yes, Joseph is gone from Sangha. I miss him—the booming voice, the fervent hallelujahs, the jangling buckets mingled with "Thank You, my Father!" I miss his praying, his nonmelodious singing, his own made-up songs.

He has gone, but I'll never forget him. My life has been enriched. He gave me a four-month lesson in "Rejoice evermore. Pray without ceasing. In everything give thanks."

15
The Night Rod Wilson Walked to Life

by JAMES R. ADAIR

At the request of the subject, his real name is not used to avoid possible embarrassment to his family in relation to his past life.—Editor

His shoulders sagging and his hands shoved deeply into his pockets, Rod Wilson could barely see the murky waters of the Chicago River from the bridge on State Street just north of Wacker Drive. At 2:00 A.M. that April night in 1971 the Chicago Loop was dead and there were lights only here and there in the nearby twin Marina Towers, for most of the apartment dwellers had long retired. The darkness seemed to fill the entire being of the handsome young black. He had decided finally that the waters of Chicago River were the answer to his problems.

Just when Rod had taken the step that started him toward such discouragement and despair would be hard to pinpoint. Being born in a black ghetto on Chicago's West Side hadn't helped. But his mother had been a God-fearing, church-going woman and had done all in her power to put Rod on the right road. As a boy he had gone regularly to Sunday school and church. But against his mother's wishes, he dropped out of church when he felt he had outgrown it—at twelve years of age.

At age fifteen he found himself letting out the stops and trying some of the things that his Sunday school teachers—and his mother—called sins. He often stayed out all night, drinking and running with the guys.

When he was sixteen, Rod became the father of a baby boy, born out of wedlock. A year or so later, a baby girl was born to him and his girlfriend. At nineteen Rod married the girl and established a home for his children.

But strangely after marriage they discovered that their interests were different in many respects. Rod became involved with pot and pills, pushing as well as using them. He was seldom home evenings, continuing to hit the fun spots with the boys. His wife was opposed to his way of life, preferring to live quietly and enjoy their children.

Rod, however, provided well, having landed a job as assistant manager of a supermarket. At twenty-one years of age, he had even purchased a home. But the things he bought his wife weren't enough, and the day came when she announced that they were through.

When she left, Rod began to drink harder. He quit his job, making spending money by pushing dope. A month after he and his wife were separated, he was arrested on a drugs charge but was soon out of jail on bond.

"I began to think about my kids and my wife the night after the court hearing, knowing that I could get a jail sentence—up to ten years, a judge had told me," Rod recalls. Deep depression overcame him as he walked the streets of downtown Chicago. Alcohol had scrambled his thoughts.

The bridge on State Street, just past Wacker Drive. The Chicago River below. The way out. In the darkness no one would see. Stand on a rail and fall into the ever-flowing water below.

In moments all his problems would be over....

Or would they? Other thoughts hammered at Rod's brain. *Jump and your problems will only begin. Man, you'll end up in the devil's hell. You're nothing but a sinner headed for hell.*

His Sunday school teaching was coming back to him. He hadn't really listened to his mother's preaching in his growing up years at home, but he knew she believed that sinners not right with God ended up in torment after death.

"God convicted me in that low state," Rod remembers. "So I walked away from the bridge. It was about 2:00 o'clock in the morning; it was very dark and no one was around. I didn't know where I was going or what I was doing. But I'm sure God was guiding me as I walked. I walked down State Street, past the Pacific Garden Mission. As I passed the mission, I saw the man inside at the reception desk. I turned around and came back and looked at him again. I had a desire to go in and talk to him, yet I didn't know what I would say or what he would say to me."

An idea hit Rod. Moments later in the Penny Arcade just south of the Eisenhower Expressway, he fished out a dime and made a phone call to the mission. He fumbled for words as the night man answered. "I was just walking by and saw you sitting there and I was wondering what you did in there." The tone of Rod's voice told Elmer Mutchler that the caller was troubled. He invited Rod to come down to talk.

"I could see that he had something that made me want to talk to him," Rod Wilson says. "Right away he asked me to pray with him. We went into the Billy Sunday Chapel right behind the recreation desk area and knelt down and prayed. Then he started talking to me about Jesus. I didn't want to hear any religious talk. But, though I only half-heartedly listened, I was touched by his compassion toward me. He quoted such verses as II Corinthians 5:17—'Therefore if any man be in Christ, he is a new creature; old things are passed away, and, behold, all things are become new.'

"All of it sounded real good, but this white man didn't know all the things I had done. So I began telling him how I had lived. I think I told him more than I had told anybody.

"Mr. Mutchler wasn't at all shocked. He concluded by assuring me that Jesus could change my life, that He had come to die for sinners, and that if I knew I was a sinner, I could be saved."

After being shown to a bed in the mission dormitory, Rod slept the remainder of the night.

After breakfast he found himself in conversation with Leonard Dare, director of the mission's Servicemen's Center. This man too talked of Christ's power to change the life of anyone who would trust Him. And like the night man, Mr. Dare evidenced compassion and love.

"That's the reason I stayed—they showed real concern and love. Not that I had any place special to go, but I hadn't come to stay," says Rod.

That night, attending the gospel service, Rod Wilson listened spellbound to convert after convert tell of discovering a joyful new life through Christ's power.

"It related to what I had heard from Elmer Mutchler and Mr. Dare, and here I was without this new life," Rod recalls. "They gave an invitation to those who wished to trust Christ and I saw people go forward, but I was nervous. I knew I needed what they were talking about, but I felt uncomfortable; I didn't know anyone."

That night in bed Rod lay thinking of his family

until he was crying. "I wanted to be with my kids and my wife and to be in my home," he says. "And I knew that that might never be. And I thought about the jail sentence and the judge—how he so sternly told me that I could get up to ten years. I lay there wondering what I was going to do. Then I thought about Elmer Mutchler at the desk. I couldn't remember his name at the time, but I could see him so vividly. The conversation we had had came back to me. He was so nice to me, though I was scared when we had talked.

"I got out of the bed and prayed. I told God I wanted to be saved. I started confessing a lot of things and crying to God to forgive me. Then I thought about something Elmer Mutchler had told me before I went to bed. He said, 'Rod, if you truly want to know the Lord Jesus, it's a gift. Jesus Christ has already done it for you.' Then finally I believed that Jesus Christ was truly my Savior, that my case was in His hands."

Today Rod Wilson glows with the knowledge that a miracle has taken place in his life. His story hasn't a lived-happily-ever-after ending, for his wife followed through and divorced him. He sees his children only at appointed intervals. But Rod has so earnestly sought to line his life up with the teachings of God's Word that he has been given a job counseling other men—new converts and others on the mission work crew, plus servicemen who visit the mission's Servicemen's Center.

Ron's conversation is interspersed in an amazing measure with Scripture. He has a rare gift for quoting both a Scripture verse and reference to buttress a point. He sometimes accompanies a mission deputation team to share his story in an area church, and longtime Christians marvel at the spiritual insight God has given this young black man in such a brief period.

A neat dresser on the job and off, Ron walks straight and tall, as though no longer carrying a heavy burden. Ask him about it and he will speak warmly, evenly. "I know God has saved me because of His own Word. Romans 10:13 tells me, 'For whosoever shall call upon the name of the Lord shall be saved.' In His Word He has given me the assurance of heaven. I think of the First Epistle of John, chapter 5, verses 9-13: 'If we receive the witness of men, the witness of God is greater: for this is the witness of God which he hath testified of his Son. He that believeth on the Son of God hath the witness in himself: he that believeth not God hath made him a liar; because he believeth not the record that God gave of his Son. And this is the record, that God hath given to us eternal life, and this life is in his Son. He that hath the Son hath life; and he that hath not the Son of God hath not life. These things have I written unto you that believe on the name of the Son of God; that ye may know that ye have eternal life, and that ye may believe on the name of the Son of God.' "

Rod would like to go to Bible school and get even better grounded in the Word of God. But as yet God hasn't shown him where to go, nor His plans for serving Him—though preaching is a possibility.

Meantime he's getting good training as he counsels men at Pacific Garden Mission. Men come to him with gripes; and Rod, remembering his days on the work crew, deals with the gripers with understanding, taking them to portions of God's Word for encouragement. Men still bound by alcoholism, the tobacco habit, or drugs find Rod a sympathetic counselor; for in time God delivered Rod from all three vices. And those with marital problems discover in Rod a man who can speak from experience concerning how God can give peace despite a broken marriage.

Rod's greatest joy comes from pointing men to his miracle-working Savior. Bob, a seventeen-year-old from a mixed-up home life, found in Rod a man who understood, who could empathize. Today he knows God as his heavenly Father because of Rod's patient counseling.

In the Servicemen's Center recently a singing, happy Rod said, "Praise the Lord," as he passed two GIs sipping coffee at a table. "What did you say?" one of the fellows asked.

"I was just saying 'Praise the Lord' because He's done great things for me. Do you know Him?" Rod asked.

Both boys talked at length with Rod and, as the conversation ended, professed faith in Rod's Savior.

As Rod Wilson would say, "Praise the Lord!" For a young black who only a relatively short time ago thought suicide was his answer, he is eternally grateful for the walk he took down South State Street that April night after deciding that suicide was not the answer to his problems.

16
Going Somewhere from Nowhere

by KATHY BAGLEY

"What's going on in there?" a gruff voice said as a fist pounded on the front door.

"Oh, no, it's the cops," Norman Johnson yelled when he opened the door.

The Johnson family had been having a get-together at Norman's grandmother's house in a black section of Philadelphia. Two of the cousins had gotten into an argument. It hadn't been serious, and now it was over; but they must've been louder than they thought. Someone had called the police.

"Everything's all right; it was just a family argument," Norman told the police. But they insisted on coming into the house.

"It's all over," Norman's grandmother said.

"You heard her!" one of the cousins said defiantly.

An officer grabbed the cousin, who jerked away and ran upstairs with the policeman after him. The other policeman called for reinforcements. Shortly three or four more policemen arrived and soon had the whole family against the wall at gun point. They started handcuffing them and taking them to the waiting paddy wagon.

They brought Norman's cousin downstairs, his head bleeding. Norman was handcuffed and led out, but apparently didn't move quite fast enough. Just before he stepped into the vehicle, he felt a thud on his head. Though he couldn't reach the wound with his cuffed hands, he knew he was bleeding.

Later, at a police station, they were booked. Next, they were taken to the hospital for X rays and stitches. Then they were held until they could see the judge the next morning.

At the hearing all charges were dropped, and Norman bears no permanent record in police files. But he does bear a permanent record of the incident in the form of a scar on his head.

Yet Norman holds no grudge against the law. (In fact, he plans to become a lawyer!) "I know that all policemen aren't bad. Just because one of them hit me on the head, I don't hate them all. They're just human beings like other people."

For Norman to be able to forgive the injustices done to him took more than a big heart. It took the grace of God. And for a person in Norman's position, it may have taken more grace than for most kids his age in the United States.

Norman grew up in a black ghetto of Philadelphia where kids band together as sort of a way of survival.

One day a friend invited Norman to go swimming at Teen Haven, a Christ-centered youth organization working in ghetto areas. They have Bible studies, films, discussion groups, camping, and personal counseling. Norman went along because he thought it might be fun.

After that, he returned with his friend to one of

the Bible studies. Norman had gone to church once in a while when he was younger, but he never gave it any thought. He believed in God, but he didn't know anything about receiving Jesus Christ.

When the counselor asked Norman if he wanted to accept Christ as his personal Savior, Norman stalled. "I'd better go home and ask my mother," he said. He never had any intention of mentioning it to her. But he did keep thinking about it, and he kept coming back to Teen Haven.

Finally, riding in a car with Teen Haven leader Doug Rogers, Norm faced the issue of Jesus Christ again. "Yeah, I want a new life," he said, and right there in the car he trusted God to forgive his sin and invited Christ into his life.

At first the guys in the neighborhood wouldn't believe he was a Christian. "You're changed, man? Saved, man? What you mean? You ain't no better'n us. You done everything we've done."

But slowly the guys got the message. It got so they tried to keep their more mischievous plans from him, and if they rumbled or broke into a store, Norm was conspicuously absent. If he found out what they had done, he had words of wisdom for them: "Man, what you doin' is all wrong."

He also told some about the Jesus way of life: "Man, you oughta start letting Jesus change you. You need love in your heart. Jesus died on a cross for your sins. He's alive now and will take your sins away." Several of Norm's friends have said yes, they would let Christ in.

There have been other changes in Norman's life. "I wasn't interested in school, I liked to mess around. Usually I got Ds and a couple of Cs. Then after I became a Christian I realized if I ever wanted to get anywhere in life I couldn't keep getting Ds." He became a Christian at the end of his eighth grade year, and in his freshman first semester, he was making As and Bs.

After he was converted, Norman accepted an invitation to ride cross country with a group of Christian bicyclers called Wandering Wheels. Until that time it had been an all-white group, but on this particular trip Norman was asked to go, along with eleven other black boys.

He needed money to fly to Washington State where the trip was to start, and for other expenses. Teen Haven and Taylor University of Upland, Indiana, which organized the trip, went together on a "scholarship" to make it possible for Norman to go.

"First we had a training period of five days when we rode about 3 miles a day. I was really sore. Then we got up to 10 miles, and then 30. The farthest we ever went was 169 miles in one day."

"It was really a great time of sharing Jesus Christ," recalls Norm. "We were asked to give our testimonies at the churches we came to, and even people along the street would stop and ask what we were doing. We'd have a chance right there to witness.

"One thing that really impressed me about the trip was the beauty of America—seeing it from a bicycle. Also, I didn't know much about whites, but I found out these Christian guys really had love for other people. If I had any prejudice before, I soon forgot about the difference in our color as we fellowshiped in the Lord. We had a great time sharing our faith."

Norman won't bring it up himself, but he was the only one of the forty-three who actually cycled the whole distance to the east coast. All of the others at some point along the way got tired, or came down with the flu, so they had to ride in the truck for a while.

Norman's ambition is to be a lawyer, a high goal for someone who started out with so much against him. He entered Taylor University in the fall of 1972. Later hopefully he will study law. "I feel I can help a lot of people; and since I'm a Christian, I have the Lord to give me the wisdom I need to help get justice for people and fight crime."

Even if he never achieves his ambition, Norman knows that his life is in God's hands. He believes Matthew 6:33, "But seek ye first the kingdom of God and his righteousness and all these things shall be added unto you."

17
No Uncertain Sound

by W. GLEN CAMPBELL

"There's a wild doctrine springing up in the Negro community—the search for a black Christ. This is something new in theology," explains King Butler, articulate black pastor of Bible Baptist Church, Kalamazoo, Michigan.

"I made a study of the Madonna and Child and found three different Negro types for three areas in Africa. In fact, every race and culture pictures Christ as similar to them. But it is idolatry for any race to think that Christ is enhanced if He looks like them. The truth is that someday all believers, regardless of race, will be conformed to His image!"

Butler believes the racial problem is going through a transitional period with the black community searching for identity. "Most of all, the Negro, as well as the white man, needs to come face to face with the problem of sin," Butler says. "He needs the solution found only in Jesus Christ."

Because Butler does not join in civil rights

marches, some Negroes feel he is a threat to their plans.

"I am not against their program," he explains, "but I feel the gospel is superior to any program of men. It must have preeminence. This causes some people to misinterpret my emphasis."

About the time of the riots in 1967, Butler thinks, the country entered a "reverse racism program" in which almost everything advanced by whites was rejected by blacks. "It is getting more difficult to communicate," he says, "because, while white people talk about law and order, most Negroes think of their bad experiences when the law was used to suppress them.

"It has become increasingly hard to reach Negroes with the gospel. They tear up tracts picturing white people, saying, 'That's the white man's religion—I don't want it!' The American Tract Society has come to the rescue with a dozen good tracts written by Negroes and picturing black people. It's going to take black men to reach black people with the gospel."

Another problem of communication between the races is that white evangelicals often mistake "soul music" for evangelistic fervor.

"Let me tell you," Butler quips, "our people can sing, saved or unsaved. It has been said that any four Negroes can make a quartet."

Butler faced some of these problems in communication when he came to Kalamazoo in 1966 to pastor a group established by an area seminary. Some in the community felt that he should be involved in civil rights marches to project the "true image" of a Negro preacher.

But in princely style Butler kept on preaching the Word of God.

Believing that he should begin at the bottom and build solidly, Butler resigned from the church and rented a room in the YMCA for a gospel service. Over one hundred people came for the first meeting. On that very day fifteen families promised to give systematically to enable the preaching of the gospel to continue to blacks in Kalamazoo. They had a week of special meetings with Bible classes in homes.

During this week Butler talked with a man who had been using LSD and was affiliated with a legalistic religion. After explaining John 1:1-14, speaking of Christ, the true Light, Butler told him that regardless of what "light" he had received through drugs, science, or religion, if he did not have Jesus Christ he was in darkness. The young man trusted Christ as Savior—the first convert in the new work. He was later instrumental in leading his wife and three couples at work to Christ.

Under God's blessing this group organized into a church in March 1968 and purchased an old church building. By September 10, 1972 the church had 161 members representing 71 families. Teacher training classes, three prayer meetings, and outdoor evangelism are strong aspects of the church ministry.

Born in Philadelphia in 1930, King came to know Christ at the age of nine when a junior church leader explained John 3:16. The realization of salvation by grace was nurtured by the "Old Fashioned Revival Hour," "Back to the Bible Broadcast," and "Radio Bible Class."

After graduation from West Philadelphia High School in 1948, King spent two years at A & T College, Greensboro, North Carolina. Unable to continue school, he worked in a hotel for several months, then took over his brother's newspaper stand. It was then he met Margaret Wilkins, a Christian girl who later became his wife.

The early years of their marriage were characterized by spiritual coldness, though they read their Bible every night and listened to gospel broadcasts faithfully. Many times Butler walked away from the known will of the Lord.

While in the hospital for surgery in 1953, Butler recalls, "The Lord began to impress on my mind that I should be obedient to His known will. I desired to follow Him wholeheartedly and prepare for the gospel ministry."

He began an earnest study of the Scofield Reference Bible and a correspondence course in Bible doctrine from Moody Bible Institute. After a year of intensive study under a teacher in his church, Butler was asked to give a trial sermon. The church recognized his gifts and gave him a ministerial license in 1956.

Two years later, King Butler left his job at the post office to serve as assistant pastor in an independent church in Philadelphia. He found many opportunities for spiritual growth at Bible conferences.

While serving as associate pastor in another Philadelphia church, he and an assistant held meetings in a Baptist church in North Carolina. Seventeen decided for Christ. A year later the church called him as pastor. He served there four years.

During this time Butler wrote articles for Christian magazines, expressing his desire to develop a monthly journal to reflect the convictions and opinions of the Negro evangelical ministry in the language and context of his people.

His home church called him to serve in their program in Philadelphia and allowed him to work with the American Sunday School Union rewriting materials in language the ghetto child could understand. He also taught part time at the Mana Bible Institute.

His Kalamazoo church has an integrated membership, with three white members in the congregation. A number of white students also come from Kalamazoo's Western Michigan University to worship.

The church sponsors a fifteen-minute evangelistic and Bible teaching radio program on Sunday evenings, which strengthens his own members and provides an outreach to the community. Speaking engagements at youth meetings, missionary conferences, and Bible school chapel services in western Michigan have widened his ministry, and his commentary for Sunday school manuals published by Urban Ministries, Inc., makes it nationwide.

Butler has no sweeping solution for the racial problem, but does have an answer for man's greater problem: "After our people find their 'identity' and gain their civil rights and more material things, they enter the mainstream of society only to face the same frustrations as white people.

"I feel that men in our black community need to realize that after all their civil rights thrust, the need for Jesus Christ is still there! I believe we need to examine Ephesians 4:8-16 where Christ gives gifted men to the church 'for the perfecting of the saints, for the work of the ministry, for the edifying of the body of Christ.'

"With this God-given division of labor in our churches, we will accomplish the Scriptural idea of making 'increase of the body unto the edifying of itself in love.' We don't need a designation of Christ as black or white. Rather, all of us, black and white, need the transforming grace of God to meet the basic need of all men—the forgiveness of sin!"